919.73
GHI

Turtle Island

SERGIO GHIONE

Turtle Island

A JOURNEY TO BRITAIN'S
ODDEST COLONY

Thomas Dunne Books
St. Martin's Press ⚏ New York

THOMAS DUNNE BOOKS.
An imprint of St. Martin's Press.

www.stmartins.com

Library of Congress Cataloging-in-Publication Data

Ghione, S.
   [Isola della tartarughe. English]
   Turtle Island: a journey to the world's most remote island / Sergio Ghione; translated by Martin McLaughlin.
     p. cm.
   ISBN 0-312-31095-1
   1. Ascension Island (Atlantic Ocean)—Description and travel. 2. Sea turtles—Ascension Island (Atlantic Ocean) 3. Ghione, S.—Travel—Ascension Island (Atlantic Ocean) I. McLaughlin, M. L. (Martin L.) II. Title
   F3030.3.G4713 2003
   919.7'3—dc22   2003058453

First published in Italy as *L'isola della tartarughe: Viaggio ad Ascensione* by Editori Laterza

First English translation published in Great Britain as *Turtle Island: A Journey to Britain's Oldest Colony* by Allen Lane, the Penguin Press

First U.S. Edition: December 2003

10 9 8 7 6 5 4 3 2 1

a mio padre

There is something about a small island that satisfies the heart of man.

RONALD M. LOCKLEY
Islands around Britain, 1945

Turtle Island

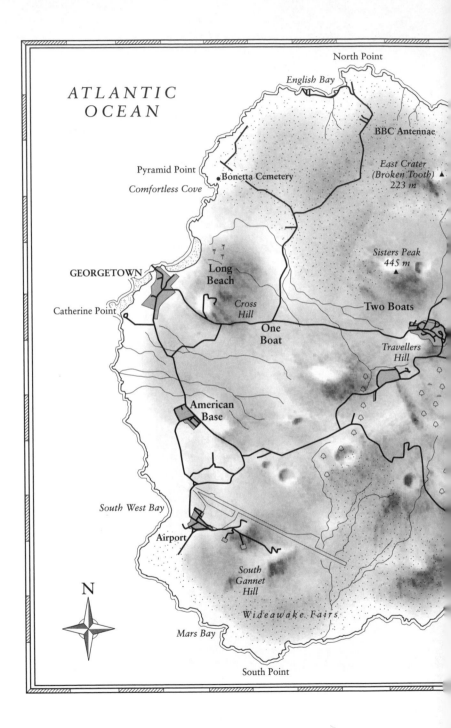

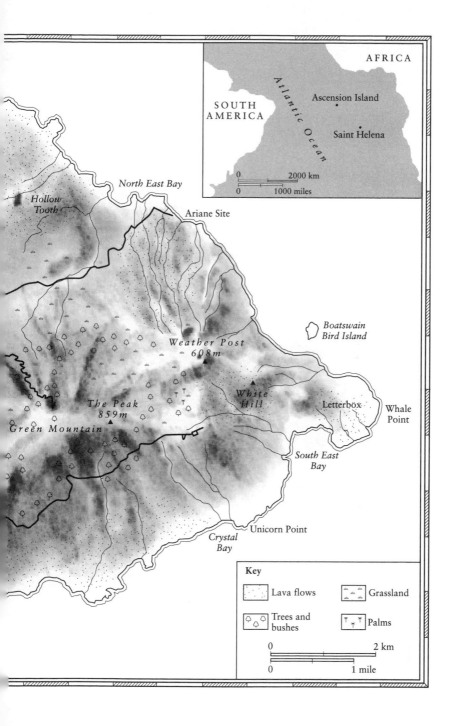

AFRICA

SOUTH
AMERICA

Atlantic Ocean

Ascension Island

Saint Helena

0   2000 km
0   1000 miles

North East Bay

Hollow
Tooth

Ariane Site

Boatswain
Bird Island

Weather Post
608m

White
Hill

Letterbox

Whale
Point

The Peak
859m

Green Mountain

South East
Bay

Unicorn Point

Crystal
Bay

Key

Lava flows

Grassland

Trees and
bushes

Palms

0   2 km
0   1 mile

Acknowledgements

I would like to mention here some people to whom I am deeply grateful: first of all, my daughters, Anna and Silvia, who forced me to carry out this project which I had unwisely revealed to them; my parents, Gabriella and some friends who had the patience to read my manuscript either in its entirety or in part and who gave me valuable advice (Paolo, Lauretta, Armando, Enza, Marirosa, Mauro, Michael, Nayva, Nino, Ruth); Francesco Orlando, Armando Petrucci and Luigi Donato for their encouragement, and Enrico Alleva for his support; Roberto Santacroce and above all Floriano Papi for having corrected countless errors: they are professors, and my incursions into their subjects bordered on rashness. The mistakes that remain are mine alone.

Prologue

'Hi, Sergio, it's Floriano. I tried to contact you at the hospital but you had already gone. I've got some good news for you. Phone me when you have a minute.'

Some months had passed since Floriano Papi had told me he was trying to go to Ascension Island; then there was no further mention of it. Floriano is a university professor, one of the top world experts on the movement and orientation patterns of marine animals, and has been a friend of my father's since his university days. Nowadays he is more my friend: we have the same hobbies (painting, chess), and we also have a series of research projects in common.

Floriano has just managed – along with other colleagues of his in the same age group – to block an attempt to make him retire even though in actual fact he has reached the legal retirement age. By doing so, he has also succeeded in wringing another two years of work out of his university and, despite his age, he maintains a healthy and at times even dangerous passion for his work.

Lately his research has centred on marine turtles, those amazing animals that live in the warm seas of the world and are able to carry out enormously long voyages in the open sea before arriving, with incredible precision, at their final destination. In order to study turtles Floriano, along with Paolo Luschi, a researcher from his institute, has been several times to Malaysia and South Africa. But the most fascinating place for studying marine turtles remains Ascension Island.

Ascension Island is in the middle of the Atlantic Ocean, just south of the Equator. A British colony, it is perhaps the most remote island in the world: to the south-east the nearest piece of land to it is 800 miles away, the island of St Helena, under whose administrative jurisdiction Ascension lies. To the north, the coast of Liberia on the African continent is about 1,000 miles away. Westwards, at a distance of 1,400 miles, is the most easterly point of Brazil and the city of Recife. And to the east, some 2,000 miles away, lies Luanda, the capital of Angola. To the south it is open sea all the way to the Antarctic.

For any Italian who, like me, is fascinated by these facts, it is as if the nearest landmass to Rome was a small island in the Eastern Mediterranean somewhere near Rhodes; and as if all around Rome there was nothing but sea all the way to Copenhagen (in the north), to Baku on the Caspian Sea (to the east), to the mid-Atlantic halfway between Portugal and the Azores (to the west) and South Africa (to the south).

Every year the marine turtles come to Ascension Island. This is the green turtle, or if you prefer its Latin name, the *Chelonia mydas*. As a rule, they do not live around the island, but come there to lay their eggs. From January to May, they land in their thousands. Even today the way they manage to find an island so small and remote in the middle of the ocean, apparently without any points of reference, is still a mystery. And it is this mystery that is the object of our research mission: in order to begin to understand something of it, we want to chart the routes taken by some of the turtles on their way back, by attaching an electronic radio transmitter on to the back of their shells – or their carapace, which is the more correct name for the turtle's shell – so that we can follow their itinerary via the satellite to which the radio sends its signal.

Floriano and Paolo have found a British partner, a marine

biologist who is also interested in turtles, and who has already been to Ascension some years ago. Along with him they have presented a research proposal, which has now just received approval for funding.

This was in fact the news that Floriano had for me when I called him back. Yes, the proposal had been approved, they were going to Ascension Island, and I could go too, if I was willing to share expenses.

I could hardly believe it. Some months later – the end of April – I am on the coach from Gatwick to Oxford, to join Floriano and the others, and then to leave with them, that very evening, for Ascension Island.

Once a friend of mine confided in me that he had a crazy passion for bridges. Not just as objects (though he has a wonderful photograph collection of bridges), but also, I believe, for their evocative power. My friend is Jewish and perhaps it is no accident that this somewhat secretive passion is for something which allows barriers to be overcome, facilitates the exchange of peoples, goods, ideas: a bridge represents a successful challenge against an obstacle.

My own passion, on the other hand, has always been for islands, another kind (in certain respects an opposite kind) of geographical-metaphorical entity. So when Floriano told me one day that he was trying to get to Ascension Island, I immediately blurted out that that was one of my dreams in life. I did not tell him the whole truth, but I was not far from it. For instance, I knew reasonably precisely where Ascension was. Just as I also knew reasonably well where the Cook Islands are, the Hebrides, the Marquesa Islands, Tristan da Cunha, Pitcairn Island and many more. These are enthusiasms which youngsters develop in early adolescence (from reading *The Odyssey, Robinson Crusoe, Treasure Island* . . .), though in my case it probably happened even earlier, when I was still a young child.

3

I remember my father, when I was three or four years old, reading me every evening a few pages from Jules Verne's *The Mysterious Island*. I have never read that book myself – and I don't feel any desire to. I prefer to cherish the vague, fable-like memories of that story about a group of people who had been shipwrecked, I think: there was a child, perhaps, and there was definitely a dog, and they had fetched up by good fortune on the eponymous mysterious island which had no inhabitants but was full of clues that suggested a human presence. In the end the human turned out to be, if I'm not mistaken, the famous Captain Nemo back from his *Twenty Thousand Leagues under the Sea*.

Of Ascension Island, I knew very little, only some indistinct recollections dating back to the Falklands War. Ascension Island often cropped up in the regular news bulletins because it acted as a staging post for the British forces, but its appearance remained hazy as rigid censorship had been imposed on television images.

I was left with a vague and unsatisfied curiosity for that island.

I

In the long winter months before our departure, I did everything I could to become well-informed about Ascension. But there was very little information to be had about that far-flung island in the middle of the Atlantic. However, on the Internet, I did manage to discover that Ascension is a volcanic island, with a surface area of around sixty square miles (more or less a third of the size of the island of Elba). Poor in vegetation, it is an important telecommunications centre for the British and even more important for the Americans, who have installed an airbase there and a series of missile-tracking and satellite-communication systems. There are no traces of tourism: no hotels, restaurants or public transport. It is a 'closed' island: you can only get there on military flights, with the permission of the British defence ministry. The resident population in 1989 was 1,127 inhabitants.

Nowadays those with enough time and money can find a tourist package to take them to *almost* anywhere in the world – from the Galapagos Islands to the Kamchatka peninsula, from the Antarctic to Mongolia, from the North Pole to Easter Island – but not to Ascension Island. It has remained to this day one of those rare outposts which are off limits to any tourist circuit, however exotic, alternative or expensive.

But what am *I* going to do on Ascension for a month? I was wondering about this on the coach which took me, at the end of April, from Gatwick to Oxford, where Floriano and Paolo had been staying for several days attending a conference. The boundless euphoria of the early period, just after the news broke, had lasted for several months: I had told everyone about it countless times, so much so that my friends and colleagues began to tease me about it.

Then, gradually, as the moment of departure got nearer, my enthusiasm declined. I almost could not bear to admit this, not even to myself. I was reminded of an aphorism I had read many years previously. It was by a writer from Vienna, Marie von Ebner-Eschenbach, and in my memory it went more or less like this: 'I had had so much pleasure looking forward to the event which was meant to happen. However, in the end the event did not take place. But why should I now be in despair? Why can I not be satisfied with the happiness I had been given by thinking it would happen?'

Why could I not then be content with what might come about but had not happened? Although, in the end, this was a small step for me, it was still a step into the unknown: I felt that behind these thoughts of mine lurked my own failure of nerve. Making the dream of a lifetime come true is no small matter, and my own insecurities now began to gather together into a mass. But another voice inside me said: '*Hic Rhodus hic salta* (This is Rhodes, jump here).' The phrase comes from Aesop's fable about the boastful traveller, who claims to have jumped an amazing length on the island of Rhodes; the man listening to him says: 'Fine, if you managed to do it in Rhodes, now do it here. Pretend that this is Rhodes, jump here.' Rhodes. Another island!

As I mulled these things over, the coach whisked me through the English countryside. Under the clear April sky, dotted with clouds, ran the undulating expanses of green fields in springtime: hedgerows, flocks of sheep dotted over the fields, villages of little red-brick houses with their square windows surrounded by broad white window-frames, and slate roofs. This was the magical landscape of southern England.

As soon as I arrived in Oxford, my misgivings vanished. Paolo was waiting for me at the bus station. The weather had changed: it was now windy and cold. Floriano had taken refuge in a bar and immediately started to devour the Italian newspaper I had bought a few hours previously, on leaving Italy.

Brize Norton, just outside Oxford, is the air base from which the twice-weekly flight for the Falkland Islands leaves, its only stopover being Ascension Island. There are no scheduled civilian airline flights to the island. To get to the little airport we took one of those typical black, square English taxis, which look so strange to us. At the wheel was an imperturbable Pakistani driver. He did not bat an eyelid at our bulky jumble of luggage. In fact we managed, though not without some difficulty, to load everything into the taxi, including 'the mummy'. This was a bag, as long and wide as a grown man, which contained the dismantled pieces of a 'turtle cage' that had been built in Floriano's institute. It was for holding the turtles while we attached the radio transmitters to them.

The evening traffic heading away from Oxford gradually thinned out; we could see the open country, then the village of Brize Norton and finally the air base. Waiting for us at the entrance was our colleague Graeme Hays. He is a marine biologist who works in one of the Welsh universities, and who has already spent three months on Ascension Island, five years ago. He is thirty years old, the same age as Paolo, but he looks little older than a young lad.

The checks at the entrance are swift and rather perfunctory for a military base, considering all the problems the British have had with Ireland. However, on the back of the entry permit issued to us there is written in bold letters:

STAY ALERT – STAY ALIVE

We did not have a clear idea of the best way to stay alert, but we all agreed on the desirability of staying alive; so each of us indulged in his own particular superstitious rituals. We were then accompanied to the airport itself. 'What's this?' asked a severe-looking military policeman on guard at the entrance, pointing to the mummy. 'A cage for turtles,' we explained. Paolo and I, one in front, the other behind, were carrying the contraption between us. The policeman did not really appreciate the funny side of the spectacle and Graeme had to intervene quickly.

However, in the end we did manage to check in all our luggage, including the mummy, without too much difficulty. I looked at the list of flights on the screen: Cyprus (delayed for twenty-four hours), Dubai, Ascension Island – Mount Pleasant (Falklands), Gibraltar. These are the last few British overseas bases that remain.

The waiting room is empty and undecorated, with just a few photographs of military planes on the walls, but it gradually fills up, though not with the usual passengers you find in most airports in the world. These are nearly all young men, soldiers in civvies. There are just a few women: some of them have a rather masculine look and are not very interesting, but others, despite their military bearing, are quite pretty and intriguing. Most people are smoking, chatting away quietly, and nearly everyone is holding a can of beer. Every now and again the loudspeaker announces something or pages somebody. The tone and content of these announcements tell us that we are in a military environment. It is not the usual seductive female voice of airport announcers: it has the clipped, brief timbre of a male voice. When they announce what items are not allowed there is a clear statement of the consequences of any violation of prohibitions. For instance, it is forbidden to take alcohol on board: anyone caught doing so will be subject to disciplinary measures. As we queue to board the plane, I put on my Australian 'Crocodile Dundee' hat, which I bought in Melbourne a few years ago, but I'm instantly rebuked: suitable clothing for the flight does not include cowboy hats. I have to carry it in my hand.

By now it is night, and outside the building we find waiting for us, in the glare of the airport lights, the huge white Tristar with the RAF insignia. The insignia looks like that of the French Air Force. This is a peculiar tendency of the British, to have different flags and insignia for different things: the Union Jack for the United Kingdom, a separate flag for England, Wales and Scotland, a different flag again for the Merchant Marine (all red, with the Union Jack in the corner), another one for the Royal Navy, and this emblem of three concentric circles, red, white and blue, for the Royal Air Force, but its colours seem more suitable for the French Air Force.

From the outside the plane resembles a civilian aircraft, but once inside it is clear that it is very different: the style is much more austere and uniform, with no division into different classes. At the front a whole row of seats has been removed and replaced by what look like strange trestles. Later on, when the plane has taken off and I can get up to wander around, I will discover what they really are: stretcher-carriers.

Take-off. For a short while I follow from the plane window the criss-crossing of yellow-orange street-lights underneath us: in the night they look like fine filigree threads. Then everything disappears beneath the clouds. Ahead of us stretches an eight-hour flight.

2

As always in aeroplanes, I slept little and badly. I ate, drank, watched a bit of a film, and soaked up the usual strange atmosphere of a night-time flight: many of the passengers are asleep, some are reading, others are talking quietly. In the semi-darkness a strange intimacy seems to come over us. But this flight was also very different from other nocturnal flights. It took some time for it to dawn on me: there were hostesses, but they behaved totally naturally, like normal people, not wearing a permanent smile.

It is always exciting seeing the sunrise from a plane. I suddenly notice that outside the window the darkness is not total. There is a faint line of light on the horizon, which is now beginning to take on an orange tinge. Above it a thin streak of white light appears, which towards its upper level shades into a beautiful light blue colour, and this in turn, still further up, swiftly shifts into an intense dark blue, which then merges with the darkness of the night. Below the plane the first light of dawn allows us to make out a weird, wide carpet of murky grey clouds, full of extraordinary peaks of lighter coloured cloud-flakes separated by dark, twisting furrows. The pilot reports that we are beginning our descent towards Ascension Island. All the passengers pronounce it 'asénshon', inverting our Italian way of pronouncing the two s-sounds in the word ('ashensióne').

The noise of the engines changes as the plane loses height,

comes through the clouds and throws all of us into the usual
terrifying moments of compulsory private panic at the inevitable turbulence. I notice the sea, leaden in colour and deserted.
The Tristar veers and leans on its side and suddenly a strip of
coastline appears, dark and purple in colour, in the grey light
of early morning. For a second, before the plane regains its
horizontal position, I catch a glimpse of a large stretch of the
coastline, wrapped in wisps of grey clouds. My excitement is
running high.

The idea of islands had fascinated me right from when I was
very small, stimulating as it did my child's imagination into
mysterious travels. These magical places had then become a
focus of imagined exploration and discovery, but also of
escape. A corner of the world, perhaps the only corner, where
utopia was not only a theoretical notion but also a potential
reality. Other layers had settled over these brief and confused
imaginings that were rooted in the past. I recall, for instance,
the first words I had come across on the Ascension site, when
I was surfing the Internet: 'It is a volcanic island, rugged, arid
and inhospitable.'

As with all landings, when I manage to secure a window seat,
I stay glued to the window looking out. The sea comes closer
and closer to us (will the plane make it this time?), but at the
last minute land appears and then, immediately afterwards,
there is the runway. The plane descends again and, with a few
bumps, makes its landing. The landscape which has briefly
flashed before us, in the uncertain light of early morning, while
the engines make their final roar before subsiding into near
silence, is disconcerting. There is something not quite right.
    There is nothing.
    No trees, no bushes, not even a blade of grass. Only the
runway, and all around it the colour of the earth, an intense,
deep brick-red. Then, as the Tristar still speeds across it

braking, on the right, just next to the runway, the ground seems to rear up as though the plane is entering a huge canyon. Halfway up this, and quite close by, I see a succession of white and blue lights which in civilian airports mark the perimeter of the runway. Above them, there is a fleeting glimpse of a huge white radar dish, and just beyond it a second, even bigger. By now the plane is almost at a standstill. It has reached the end of the runway and is turning. My eyes now take in the other side. No houses, no roads, not even the slightest sign of life: only earth, stones and strange contours. In the distance a desolate, ghostly mountain stands out against the pearl-coloured sky, wrapped in wisps of cloud like smoke steaming from its entrails. Now I understand Don Quixote and his windmills – he immediately comes to mind. In a hollow between two plateaux, four enormous wind generators appear, distant and threatening, with their blades slowly turning. Giants stationed there to guard this desolate land, they ceaselessly turn their huge, absurd arms.

By now the plane has reached its stand. The loudspeaker announces that the stopover at Ascension will be forty-five minutes and that there is the possibility of rain. As soon as I reach the top of the steps, I feel the usual sudden but pleasant sensation of the hot, humid wind that engulfs you when you arrive in the tropics.

We go across the runway on foot, still dazed. I look around: there are no other aircraft: the airport is empty. But opposite us (and it is a small relief to see that there is somebody there) are stationed the fire-brigade truck, an ambulance and other emergency vehicles, all with their yellow lights winking. We are herded towards a small cordoned-off area, behind which stands the low terminal building. A notice greets us: 'Welcome to RAF Ascension.' Soon after they escort us into a little waiting-room along with three or four other passengers. The others all stay outside, sitting on the benches in the cordoned-off area, before being called to continue their journey (another eight hours) towards the Falklands. It is the end of April: in Europe spring is in full bloom, but here, even though it is only early morning, you can tell it is going to get very hot; in Port Stanley, in the Falklands, the first snow has fallen – it delayed the departure of the last plane to take off last week.

Lunar, that's it, a lunar landscape: the idea suddenly comes to me as I walk across the runway. Just for a second I can feel that sense of completeness that comes with even the slightest intuition. I daren't risk photographing or videoing anything. I feel intimidated and am afraid of breaking heaven knows what military regulation, and running the risk of instant expulsion from the island. My God, where have I ended up?

Ascension Island has always impressed its few visitors on first impact. A few years ago, the English journalist Simon Winchester described his travels through the last British colonies (or 'dependent territories' as they are officially known). The title of his book was *Outposts*, with the ironic subtitle: *The Empire on Which the Sun Never Sets*. Winchester too came by military aircraft to Ascension. But he had the privilege of being on the flight-deck with the pilots:

A smooth American voice came on the line. 'Ascot two zero one niner – good day, sir. Welcome to Ascension Island. Wind eight knots. Clear skies at the field. No traffic. Come right on in, and have yourself a nice day!' And so we slid down to the glidepath of the loneliest of ocean way-stations, until with a bump and a puff of iron-red cinder-dust we touched down on board and I, who alone in the cockpit had never been here before, thought we had landed on the surface of the moon.

3

Ascension Island was discovered by Portuguese navigators looking for a sea-route to the Indies. They were trying to break the Muslim (and Venetian) stranglehold on trade by discovering a route which did not entail the crazy notion of going round the world in the opposite direction. At the end of the fifteenth century, at the instigation of the Portuguese monarchy, several expeditions were launched, bound for the South Atlantic in order to find a sea-route to the Indian Ocean and the Orient.

The idea that Africa could be circumnavigated was known even to the ancient Greeks. Herodotus tells us in his *Histories* that Neco II, Pharaoh of Egypt from 615 to 595 BC, had several Phoenician ships sail from Egypt into the Erythrean (or Red) Sea towards the Southern (or Indian) Ocean. When autumn came, the men moored the ships, prepared a piece of land to plant grain and waited for it to ripen. Once they had harvested it, they left. They continued to do this for the next two years, and at the end of the third year, they rounded the Pillars of Hercules (the Straits of Gibraltar) and arrived home. In their accounts of the voyage they reported that when they sailed round Libya (Africa) they always had the sun on the right-hand side.

This was a tale, Herodotus notes nearly two hundred years later, 'that for my part I do not believe [. . .] even though others maybe do'. It is not entirely clear what Herodotus meant when he said that those Phoenician sailors had the sun on their right-hand side. The most likely hypothesis is perhaps this: those who travelled by sea in those days relied heavily on the position of the sun and knew that, when circumnavigating any island, if the sun at midday was on the right of the ship as it went down one coastline, then it would naturally be on the other side of the ship when they were on the other side. This would have been expected even in circumnavigating Africa, which the Phoenicians did in a clockwise direction. Consequently, having gone along the Mediterranean coast with the midday sun on their right, at a certain point in their voyage they would have expected to find it on their left. The fact that in the Phoenicians' account this did not happen, made this story in Herodotus' eyes highly unlikely, but this is no longer so for us, who know nowadays how to explain this phenomenon: the ships had crossed the Equator, and from that point on, the sun at midday was to the North not the South. Perhaps what makes this story credible is the very admission by Herodotus that he does not believe it, but that he is recounting it all the same since that was how it had been reported to him.

Back to the Portuguese explorers. Some of their names have been entirely forgotten, like that of Diogo Cão, who in 1481 sailed beyond the estuary of the river Congo and traces of whom recently have been found there. Others are more famous, such as Bartolomeu Dias, who in 1488 rounded the Cape of Good Hope without seeing it because he was blown too far out to sea by a storm. He just continued sailing south until he noticed that there was no more coast to the east. But Dias did not go much beyond the Cape, which he himself named, on his return journey, the Cape of Storms, though it was subsequently renamed Cape of Good Hope by his king, John II of Portugal, who clearly knew something about the evocative power of names. It seems that in reality Dias was not very skilled in dealing with men, since he was unable to persuade or even force – which was basically the same thing – his crew to continue their voyage, particularly the officers, and these are the men who count on these occasions.

Nine years later, in July 1497, Vasco da Gama also set out from Lisbon: by then the situation had become urgent because Columbus, in the employ of the Spanish, had already returned from his travels. In order to avoid both the currents along the African coast and being becalmed on the Equator, da Gama chose a more seaward route. He was lucky: after little more than four months he managed to round the Cape of Good Hope, and after a voyage lasting ten months he reached Calicut on the south-west coast of India, the main centre for spices. Da Gama returned home to Lisbon two years after setting out, in September 1499.

The route to the Indies was open. In 1500 Pedro Àlvares Cabral set sail: following the same idea as Da Gama, he ventured into the South Atlantic and discovered the coasts of Brazil before retracing his route back to Africa, rounding the Cape of Good Hope, where Bartolomeu Dias, the captain of one of the expedition's ships, met his end, and reaching the Indies.

Expedition followed expedition in constant succession: the next year, 1501, another group of ships set sail sent by the Portuguese king, captained by the Spaniard Juan da Nova Castella. Fifty years later the Portuguese historian João de Barros reported that these ships, 'after sailing eight degrees to the south of the Equator, discovered an island to which they gave the name Conception'. There is no doubt that this was Ascension Island: it lies at 7° 57' south, and it is the only island in the middle of the Atlantic at that latitude. On his return journey from India he then discovered Saint Helena.

It is unlikely that Da Nova actually landed on Ascension. The island was uninhabited, and it would stay that way for some considerable time after that. Nor did Alfonso of

Albuquerque land there either, when he sailed by two years later, perhaps on Ascension Day itself. The earlier name of Conception also came from the religious calendar. The idea of giving a newly discovered island a name deriving from the feast-day on which it was discovered was quite common: Easter Island, Christmas Island (in fact there is more than one of them) and even Saint Helena itself reflect this practice. As for Albuquerque, he was responsible for more famous exploits than naming – or rather renaming – a tiny, remote island in the middle of the Atlantic: he went on to become Viceroy of the Indies, capturing Goa on the India coast, which remained a Portuguese colony until 1961, when Nehru, in a surprise move, chased the Portuguese out. He occupied important strategic positions like the island of Ormuz, at the entrance to the Persian Gulf, the island of Socotra, at the entrance to the Gulf of Aden and therefore also to the Red Sea, and Molucca, on the Malaysian peninsula, near what is today Singapore. He really laid the foundations for the Portuguese presence in the Indian Ocean, and was in effect the real initiator of Western domination in the Orient.

In 1506 Albuquerque set sail again from Lisbon bound for the Indies. The admiral commanding his fleet was Tristão da Cuña, who discovered the island that bears his name in that very year, the third island which makes up, along with Saint Helena and Ascension, the British colony in the South Atlantic.

4

They have come to collect us in a minibus and a jeep with a trailer into which we fling our luggage, including the mummy. I notice that in the little airport car park the space next to us is private: 'Reserved for HH the Administrator,' says the notice. I presume that HH stands for 'His Honour': we *are* in one of the last British colonies.

'Are you a television team?' I am asked by the black lad loading our luggage. He is thin, dressed in a tee-shirt, with dark skin, though he does not have African features. Furthermore, his eyes are almond-shaped and blue. He is mild-mannered and very good-looking.

Our initial reaction is one of mistrust: 'No,' I reply rather brusquely, 'we are scientists.' He is the first Saint Helenian – or 'Saint', as they are called – that we have met. Beside him is an Englishman, a round man with reddish hair: he is in charge, but he too is in tee-shirt and shorts. Later we will discover that they are policemen. Some days later we will run into them again in the police station, dressed in impeccable London bobby uniform: black trousers, white shirt, and peaked cap with the line of black and white checks.

Lining the road away from the airport are a few palm trees which remind me that we are in the tropics. Then whatever vegetation there is disappears and we find only stones, the odd bush and bare and dusty earth, which in some places looks like black gravel.

On the few occasions we meet another car (it's still early morning) our driver waves hello, and gets a wave back. This is a habit that we too will soon acquire. Things that in our cities are impossible, here have a real purpose. Just like in the mountains, or in a village or when you ride through the countryside on a bike. On the whole island there are fewer than a thousand people, all of whom know each other in one way or another, so when they meet, either on foot or in cars, they wave hello. So it is not just politeness. Perhaps it is an indication that they are the ones who have got it right.

The journey from the airport to Georgetown is short. We are taken to our lodgings. It is called 'The Islander Hostel' and, at first sight, it looks as if it is one of the few two-storey brick buildings in Georgetown. It has about a dozen big, comfortable rooms, which give out on to two broad verandas that look on to the two longer sides of the building. The windward side, which is on the same side as the street, is protected by glass: as we will soon learn, here the wind never stops; it blows continuously and always from the same quarter. The leeward side opens on to a little square of black gravel, surrounded by some low prefabricated buildings through which one can see the sea in the distance.

Once our bags have been offloaded – it is always Graeme who leads us and who knows what to do – we feel we should introduce ourselves to the Administrator, but in all probability he is not yet at work. So we decide first to sort out the legal formalities. The police station is only a few minutes' walk away, a white building, on one level only, with a portico. On either side of the entrance stand two cannon shells which act as barriers. They are painted blue, and beside them on the wall is a notice in the same blue paint with the inscription:

ST HELENA POLICE
ASCENSION DETACHMENT
POLICE OFFICE
GEORGETOWN

The interior of the police office is simple: a desk, a radio transmitter, a megaphone and, on the walls, a map of the island and a large and decidedly out-of-date photograph of the Royal Family, including a smiling Princess Diana. We pay the residence tax, as our passports are stamped: IMMI-GRATION/25 APRIL 1997/ASCENSION. I stare long and hard at the stamp, as if it were some kind of trophy.

I ask where we can leave our money (we still need to pay for a month's board and lodging). Has the police station got a safe? The black lad in the tee-shirt, who has just stamped my passport, looks at me in bewilderment: he does not understand, then he relaxes into a smile of amusement. We can leave our money in our bedroom quite safely: there is no problem, no one robs anything here. Later we discover that here, when people get out of their car, they leave it open with the keys in the ignition. No one ever locks their house at night. And we too, after the first few days, will learn to leave our rooms open without worrying about money or anything else we have.

I squint into the room next to the police office. It houses the island's courtroom: in the darkness I can make out the judge's chair in the middle, and on either side are the two desks for the prosecution and the defence; against one wall leans a notice which I presume is placed outside on the few occasions when the court is sitting, with the words: 'Silence: Court in Session'. Right next to the police station is the Administrator's Office: he is the chief authority on the island, subordinate only to the Governor, who has his residence on Saint Helena. The Administrator is a short, round and ruddy man with a limp, and a small red beard covering his chin. A kind and polished individual, he regales us with a ceremonial welcome to the island. He asks about our project and displays some interest: one of his hobbies is natural history and he is writing a short monograph, of which he shows us the proofs, on the Ascension Island turtles. But he is quick to point out, as if to avoid any misunderstanding, that he is no scientist. Floriano tells him about his previous experiences in Malaysia and South Africa, about how we had used the radio transmitter system to work out the turtles' routes for thousands of miles.

Our brief audience is over. The Administrator asks us to sign his Visitors' Book, then bids us farewell saying that he would invite us to dinner one evening in his residence, 'in the cool, on top of the mountain'. We emerge back on to the street dazzled by the early morning sun. We have completed all the formalities. For the next month we are Ascensionites.

5

On the jetty, with its wide view of the sea, the sense of isolation that hits me is overwhelming: the infinite distance facing us and all around us; the endless blue of the sky, and scattered over it enormous fantastically shaped white clouds that tower above us; the limitless green of the sea stretching to the far horizon and who knows how far beyond; the wind whining tensely; the idea that no matter which direction you go in, there is nothing for thousands of miles but sea and sky.

I am reminded of Manaus, the city surrounded by the forest, in the centre of Amazonia. My hotel there was on the river, on the edge of the city. Late one evening I had gone out for a walk. Behind me there was a sliver of brightness in the sky: it was the city with its noise and lights; but everywhere else, all around, stretching out endlessly lay the invincible realm of darkness and mystery, in which we were immersed totally and unconditionally.

However, the spectacle near the shore soon manages to dispel the initial feelings of estrangement: all around there is an incredible whirling of birds. They are not seagulls; there are no gulls on the island. My friends, like the good zoologists they are, inform me that they are booby birds. Later a fisherman will explain to us that when the tuna and other big fish approach the shore, the shoals of blue fish escape to seabeds nearer the surface and then become prey for the boobies. Hundreds of these birds swirl above the sea, then suddenly plunge down headlong, like arrows fired into the water.

Beside us are a few other spectators, looking towards the sea and enjoying the sight of the booby birds. Some of them are white (British), others black (Saint Helenians). No one seems to be in any particular hurry.

We too are in no hurry to discover everything immediately. We have a whole month ahead of us. I have travelled a fair bit across the globe, but always at a different pace: staying a maximum of two or three days in any one place, and devoting the majority of time to my work. And even on holiday, who can afford more than a couple of weeks? But on Ascension the temporal perspective expands incredibly, like the summer holidays when you were at school: the time you have ahead of you, which separates you from going back, is measured in weeks not days!

When the others go back to the Islander Hostel, I stay behind on the jetty: to watch the sea, the birds, the clouds, the empty white beach stretching out to the left, the rocks to the right, the green seabed visible through the transparent water and swarming with shoals of fish; and to listen to the noise of the wind, the cry of the birds, as they approach the island in flight, and the voices of two young Saint-Helenian kids, snatches of whose conversation strike my ear every now and then.

Off the coast a petrol-tanker lies moored, while closer to the island a group of fishing-boats and a single sailing boat are at anchor. A little rowing boat sets off from the yacht and heads towards the pier. From on high I watch it reach the harbour entrance directly below me: a man at the oars, a woman and two children. The kids – they must be about six or eight – jump out happily, climb quickly up the little flight of landing steps and then, like all children of that age, run off towards the beach laughing and playing. The young mother at first chases after them a little anxiously, then just lets them go. The father, who has by now moored the boat, comes up.

He too is young, blond-haired, his skin bronzed by the sun. He speaks to the two Saint-Helenians who are leaning beside me on the balustrade overlooking the sea. He has just arrived and asks what he needs to do to complete formalities. His English is correct but full of harsh guttural sounds, which I easily recognize as I know German well.

What on earth is a German doing here? I ask him directly: 'Wo kommen Sie hier?' He answers, in German, perfect German with a Bavarian cadence, that he has come from Africa, from Namibia, which up until the First World War had been a German colony, and which to this day still has a substantial German community. He cannot be more than thirty, and was born in Walvis Bay. He has always lived there: the worst place on earth, according to him, with its cold, stormy sea and its burning desert land: both of them totally hostile elements. And, as if that were not enough, there is constant fog. He was a carpenter. At a certain point – he tells me – he decided to leave. He built himself a boat, sold everything and set off. It took him three weeks to reach Saint Helena, his first stop, then another nine days to make it to Ascension. Both the wind and the weather have been kind to him, for the moment. He is heading for the Caribbean: where exactly, he does not yet know. Somewhere nice, warm and sun-lit, far from the mists of Namibia, somewhere he can go on doing what he does best: being a carpenter. I wish him good luck.

How small those distances can seem, which just a few minutes previously had seemed to me so enormous! With a tiny yacht built with his own hands, two kids, a young wife and a bit of good luck he will arrive in the Caribbean long before we get back home.

6

After its discovery by the Portuguese, someone – perhaps the Portuguese sailors themselves – left a few goats on Ascension Island, as was the custom in those days. These constituted both a food supply and a means of testing, subsequently, whether it was worth while establishing a human settlement there. Despite the scant vegetation the goats survived and multiplied, however meagrely. Nevertheless, apart from the occasional, accidental visitor, the island remained uninhabited for three centuries.

On 22 April 1701 William Dampier was shipwrecked on the island. Less famous than Sir Francis Drake, who lived a century earlier, or James Cook, who lived seventy years later, William Dampier was one of those great navigators to whom the British owe their Empire. He was a mixture of pirate, adventurer, explorer and scientist. On his way back from a voyage to the southern Indian Ocean on behalf of the Admiralty, his ship was damaged in a storm, so as soon as he sighted Ascension he tried to land. He succeeded, but his ship did not. And along with the ship, apparently, went a fabulous treasure which is still talked about even today and which some people persist in trying to track down on the island or on the seabed offshore. Dampier and his men were lucky: by following the goat-tracks they managed to discover the only water source on the island

and thus survive. Nowadays the source has dried up, but it is to this day known as Dampier's Drip.*

Who knows whether amongst the crew there was already at this date a certain Scottish sailor by the name of Alexander Selkirk. Perhaps it was on this occasion that he developed his taste for the life of the shipwrecked mariner. In any case, the fact is that, some years later, while taking part in an expedition of English ships led by Dampier, following violent disagreements with his captain, Selkirk asked to be left on the desert island of Juan Fernandez in the Pacific Ocean, 400 miles off the coast of Chile. He stayed there for four and a half years, and was rescued in 1709 by Dampier himself, who was sailing once more in those waters on his final voyage.

Selkirk returned home and wrote an account of his adventure which made him, for a brief period, quite famous. If he is remembered today it is because his memoirs provided the inspiration for another book, written shortly afterwards by one Daniel Defoe: *The Life and Strange Surprising Adventures of Robinson Crusoe of York, Mariner, Written by Himself.*

Dampier also enjoyed an adventurous life, making several voyages of discovery, some as far as the coasts of Australia and New Guinea. He also wrote a book, *A New Voyage round the World*, in which he recounted his travels and popularized the notion of an enormous southern continent: the *Terra Australis Incognita*, whose existence was already vaguely suspected by Chinese, Arab, Portuguese, Spanish and Dutch merchants and explorers, but which eventually became British.

The tiny museum on Ascension still has copies of various documents concerning Dampier, including the diary which he kept after his shipwreck and which recorded his subsequent mishaps. He spent five weeks on Ascension. Once back home,

---

* The wreck was recently found by an Australian diving team some 100 metres off the shore at the Long Beach: they recovered a brass bell. (S. G., 2002.)

he was accused by one of his officers of maltreatment. He was found guilty, stripped of office and declared unfit in perpetuity to captain His Britannic Majesty's ships. Ten months later, however, he was setting off for the Indies, captaining the *St George*, and not before having had the honour of kissing His Majesty's hand. For in the mean time the War of Spanish Succession had broken out: the Spanish and French had become enemies of the English, so that a buccaneer who knew how to sail the southern seas in the service of the King of England had once more become useful.

Other navigators went to Ascension, amongst whom were Louis de Bougainville and James Cook, but none of them remained for anything other than a brief stay. Cook landed on the island during his voyage round the world in 1775, on his way back from the Pacific having discovered, in the South Atlantic, the South Sandwich Islands and South Georgia. Once he arrived at Ascension, he took advantage of the stop to seek out another nearby island, about which he was extremely curious: Saint Matthew's Island.

Saint Matthew's Island is the nearest landfall to Ascension, lying to the north-east of it, halfway towards the African coast: it could be found on any atlas of the world or of the Atlantic up to halfway through the nineteenth century. It has one peculiarity: it does not exist. It is a phantom island, the result of some explorer's inaccurate report or his fancy, and handed down with great conviction from cartographer to cartographer for over three hundred years. Or perhaps it really was an island which emerged and then disappeared, like another island which I will come back to shortly.

The history of phantom islands, of mysterious isles which remain in the memory of legends, really requires a chapter to itself, and has already been partly recounted: from St Brendan's Island, the home of peace, harmony and eternal youth, to the island of Buss, which some smart sailors managed to sell to the Hudson Navigation Company, and the Friesland Islands, whose products were sold by the Venetians. Not to mention the phantom islands in literature, music and poetry, from More's *Utopia* to Peter Pan's Neverland.

7

In the north-east corner of the island lies Georgetown, the capital, protected by the trade winds, and the only real landing point on Ascension Island.

Georgetown's landscape is dominated by Cross Hill, which rises up behind the town: this is a massive volcanic outcrop, covered with bare, smooth earth, and marked by irregular ridges caused by the infrequent rains. It is devoid of vegetation, apart from a single solitary tree halfway up the slope. It appears dark and majestic in the early morning, when the side that looks towards Georgetown is not yet lit up by the sun. But as the hours go by the mountain turns a deep rust-red which seems to glow like fire at sunset. A road with wide zig-zags runs across the slope: it leads to two First World War artillery pieces and to the round summit, where there is a huge cross that dates from the nineteenth century and a number of aerials built by the Americans. Cross Hill is one of the many cones of volcanic waste – or scoria cones, the term used by geologists – that are found on the island.

Beneath the hill the town stretches out, peaceful, orderly and sleepy. It consists of about thirty houses built along the main street and the three short roads that lead to the jetty, the cemetery and the beaches. Mostly low, one-storey prefabs, built in the last ten or twenty years, these are the lodgings of the Saint-Helenian workers and the houses of the British employees. Both types of building follow English suburban housing patterns and seem to be surrounded by small gardens in which grow magnificent bougainvilleas and other highly coloured tropical plants, not such an English touch.

The few buildings that are two storeys high and built of masonry date from the apogee of the colonial period: the garrison headquarters, the depots beside the jetty, and the former telecommunications headquarters, which used to link Britain with South Africa and South America, but which now has been turned into a hostel – the Islander Hostel – for the island's few visitors, amongst whom we now find ourselves.

The main square in the town – or in the capital, if you prefer – is a small, partly tarmacked square, on to which look the post office, the supermarket, and the Exiles' Club. At the back of the square stands the Administrator's Office, freshly whitewashed and surrounded by an untidy garden with a pair of trees. In the centre there stands, high and proud in the wind, the British flag.

The post office, immediately recognizable thanks to the familiar round red postbox near the entrance, is a place of considerable importance for philatelists all over the globe. Stamps which are obviously produced in Britain are transported out here, where they are franked for authenticity and are then dispatched around the world for stamp-collectors to savour (as well as to exchange and sell). Inside the small post office, a glass case displays the latest issues. For the Queen's seventieth birthday there is one showing a now elderly Elizabeth II wearing the inevitable hat and, in the background, the Church of St Mary of Georgetown (twenty pence) or the Administrator's residence (twenty-five pence) or the Exiles' Club (sixty-five pence); then there is one with the local seabirds and flora of Ascension; and another still with a most improbable Santa Claus going round the island celebrating Christmas 1995.

The supermarket is the only real shop on the island. It would be just like any other small provincial supermarket were it not for some peculiarities: for instance, the country of origin of the goods – roughly two thirds of them come from Britain, and one third from South Africa. These are the two destinations of the *St Helena*, the mail ship which comes to the island once a month.

During our time on Ascension there was no cheese. Maybe there had been a gap in supply, or consumption had suddenly gone up; but the fact remains that for more than a month it was not possible to find any kind of cheese on the island. That was what was reported by the *Islander*, the only newspaper, which comes out every Friday. For a whole month we had to forget about cheese in our lunches and dinners at the Saints' (i.e. the Saint Helenians') Mess. There was just one exception to this: the night we were invited as the Administrator's guests, in whose residence we were offered a varied and very welcome *plat des fromages*. Given his privileges, the Administrator was able to procure cheese, presumably by plane.

In the supermarket there were other signs of a mismatch between supply and demand. One whole counter was given over to products past their sell-by date, as a notice officially announced. Further on you could find the typical products for *all* the festivals of the year: Carnival had come and gone, some months previously, Easter was a month past, and there were still eight months to Christmas. And yet on display you could find little packets of Carnival confetti, Easter eggs, Christmas decorations and rockets for New Year. A notice read: 'Shop early for Christmas! Buy now, don't be caught out at the last moment!'

Just beyond the supermarket there rises a huge, square, rather dilapidated building, one of the oldest in Georgetown. Built in the colonial style, two storeys high, surrounded by a portico and crowned with a small tower, this is 'The Exiles' Club'. An old cannon beside the entrance is a reminder of its military origin: this was at one time the headquarters of the garrison commander.

The interior is now showing its many years. Through the

dusty windows on the ground floor one can make out on the inside bare rooms containing abandoned tyres, chests, rubble and dirt. On the upper floor the English still have their club, the Exiles' Club (on an island that is so far away from everything else, the name is certainly appropriate). It is a vast half-empty hall, with the bar counter in the middle and, hanging from the ceiling, two huge fans now stationary. All around, the walls speak of events that took place in a past that will never return. On two huge turtle shells hanging on the wall is the list of the British and American military commanders of the island – but the list ground to a halt many years ago. There are also yellowing photographs of Elizabeth and Philip, on their wedding day. With a little bit of imagination you could summon up a colonial atmosphere worthy of the stories of Somerset Maugham or Joseph Conrad, in this forgotten corner of the Empire, where a small group of officers and engineers and technicians would spend endless evenings drinking in terminal boredom, waited on by black servants.

As recently as five years ago, when Graeme first came to Ascension, access was denied to anyone not British (i.e. Saint Helenians). Today the Exiles' Club is theoretically open to everyone, but in fact it is closed almost every evening; and even for lunch it opens only rarely.

From the Exiles' Club the road goes down to the sea. Some grey stone buildings, a crane, scores of containers scattered around in a disorderly fashion, a couple of lorries and at the very end, squat and high against the sea, the jetty. In days gone by, there had been several attempts to build a longer one; but it would be as pointless now as then: sooner or later it would be destroyed by the rollers, the powerful ocean waves, which are stirred up by the Atlantic storms and crash against the island.

In the natural harbour, a dozen boats are anchored. These are used for fishing or for transporting people or goods from the few ships which arrive and have to lie offshore. Occasion-ally a transatlantic yacht calls in, but the Administrator's regulations state that it cannot stay more than two days. A little further offshore, about half a mile out, is the *Maersk Ascension*, the petrol tanker that supplies the island with fuel and which has now been there for many years. The ship never leaves Ascension; it is periodically refuelled by another twin-tanker and once a month it sails round the island to stretch its propellers.

8

Geologists tell us that 200 million years ago, in what they call the Triassic period, from which the most ancient fossilized forms of the sea turtles date, the geography of the earth was completely different from what it is today. The landmasses which had emerged, formed by the lighter minerals, which had risen up to the surface from the depths of the earth like buoys floating on water, had solidified in the billions of preceding years. Like gigantic rafts (geologists prefer the metaphor of plates), these huge pieces of the earth's crust had gone – and even today still go – floating away. Bumping into each other, fragmenting, joining together again, they gave rise to geographical agglomerations in imperceptibly slow but endless reconfiguration – in just the same way as the level immediately above the earth's surface, the atmosphere, is continually changing but in a faster more visible way. These are the only changes that we, with our restricted, subjective window on things, are able to note and, to a limited extent, to predict, as they shift in their small and, to our eyes, erratic oscillations.

It was at that particular time, in the Triassic era, that the newly surfaced landmasses had for the most part solidified into a single gigantic supercontinent: Pangaea. At that time Africa was joined on one side to South America, and on the other, where today we find Madagascar, to the Antarctic, Australia and India, which then was very far away from the rest of Asia. This was when for some unknown reason there began to open up in this enormous earth-raft, between that area that would later become South America and that which was destined to bear the name of Africa, a gigantic crack, which spread from south to north like a zip being unfastened, and removed Africa and later Europe from the American continent. And into the fissure that gradually opened rushed the sea. That was how the Atlantic Ocean was created.

Something similar appears to be happening today in the Red Sea and the Gulf of Aden, between north-east Africa and Arabia. All you need to do is to look at a map to realize that, just like Africa and South America, north-east Africa and Arabia are two bits of a jigsaw puzzle which were at one stage joined together but are now forever drifting apart. In a few million years the Red Sea will be a new ocean.

Geologists tell us that on the ocean bed, where a plate has started to split, the fissure deepens until it reaches that area where, thanks to the heat and the pressure, the earth is partly in liquid form. And through that crack lava begins to flow slowly and as it cools it solidifies and becomes a mass which in turn develops into a volcanic mountain chain beneath the sea. But more and more new lava continues to flow from the depths and to dilate the sides of the crack, pushing to the outside the lava that has accumulated previously. In this way the ocean floor is made to flow slowly and without interruption towards the outer sides like two enormous conveyor belts moving from the centre in opposite directions, and forcing the continents that had once been joined together further and further apart.

How fast do continents float away? Not very fast: at the Cité des Sciences et de l'Industrie at La Villette in Paris, there is a piece of (fake) wall with a crack, which has widened from the day of the museum's opening at the same speed as Africa and America today are drifting apart. The museum was opened in 1986 by Giscard d'Estaing. Today that crack is about fifteen centimetres wide and you can easily put your hand inside. Had it been the wall of a house, the house would probably have collapsed by now. Another example: the speed at which continents drift apart is roughly the same as that at which human nails grow.

In the case of the Atlantic Ocean, the central submarine mountain chain is called the Mid-Atlantic Ridge and stretches the extent of the whole ocean, from Iceland all the way down to Bouvet Island near Antarctica, where it then continues eastwards and westwards as the Indian Ridge and Pacific Ridge respectively. This system of oceanic ridges, which are thought to fit together with each other like the cracks in a broken jug, represents the biggest invisible volcanic mountain chain in the world: its length is 44,000 miles, its width 1,000 miles, and its height 2,000 miles from the seabed. It has been estimated that, if these oceanic ridges did not exist, the sea-level would be about 200 metres lower than it is.

Besides these there are also areas called (by geologists again) 'hot spots', where the earth's crust is thinner and the production of magma greater, and where actual undersea volcanoes are formed which eventually emerge from the sea and produce the volcanic islands of the oceans. This is the origin of practically all the islands in our oceans.

Resting on the slowly shifting ocean, islands are also in movement. As it moves away from the hot spot that generated it, an island usually meets one fate in the end: that of being swallowed up again. This is partly because the ocean floor on which it rests tends to sink the more the island moves away, and partly because as it recedes from the hot spot, the production of new matter, new lava, by the volcano, ceases. Sometimes an island, although it is swallowed up, leaves traces. As the volcano sinks before it disappears completely under the sea, the corals along its coasts, just underneath the water level, continue to grow upwards, first producing a coral barrier-reef, and later, when the actual volcanic island has disappeared beneath sea-level for millions of years, giving way to a thin ring which outlines the traces of the coast it once had: an atoll. This phenomenon was discovered and discussed by Darwin.

Ascension is a 'young' island: its most ancient rocks date from no more than a million years ago, and the most recent ones go back to only 600 years ago when the last great eruption took place. Beneath the sea, the slopes of the volcano continue to descend for another 3,200 metres. Its base, which rests on the ocean floor, is thought to have a diameter of around forty miles. Of this gigantic volcano only the highest and most recent peak appears above land: nothing is known of the part beneath the sea.

Other tales of volcanic islands are worth a brief mention.

On 27 August 1883, the volcano on the little island of Krakatoa, in the Sunda Strait, between Java and Sumatra, erupted. The explosion was heard as far away as Perth in Australia, some 2,000 miles away, and the tidal wave which it caused claimed 36,000 victims and was felt even in South America and in Hawaii.

On 8 May 1902 the volcano known as La Pelée ('bald head'), in Martinique, erupted. Apparently it was the eruption that would boast the highest number of victims in the whole of the newly dawned twentieth century. It destroyed the city of Saint-Pierre, killing all its 36,000 or so inhabitants, apart from one: a black man who was a cobbler and who was being held in the prison basement awaiting execution.

On 14 November 1963, the sailors on board a fishing boat a few miles off the south coast of Iceland noticed that the sea waters were unusually stormy: however, this was not a storm approaching but the beginning of an underwater volcanic eruption. It lasted four years: when it was over, a new island had been added to geographical maps. This, the youngest island on the planet, by the name of Surtsey, was called after Surtur, the giant who, in Norse mythology, will proclaim the end of the world and destroy it by fire on the day of the Last Judgement.

It is a small island, comparable in size and distance from the coast to Gorgona, off the Tuscan coast. It has been declared a national park and from that time scientists have been studying its development. The first living creatures to arrive were birds, then crabs. By 1987 there were twenty-four species of plants already on the island. Thirty years or so later, its destiny is still uncertain: if there are no more eruptions, Surtsey will finally disappear several thousands of years from now, eroded by storms, and finished off by the sea and the wind.

But Surtsey has already lost its record as earth's youngest island. The most recent one, if still others have not emerged while this book was being written, is called Lahtayikee, and it was born in March 1996 in the Tonga Islands archipelago, in the Pacific Ocean, north of New Zealand.

Finally, to return to more familiar latitudes, the island of Ferdinandea should be mentioned: in 1831 it popped out of the sea in the Sicilian Channel between Sciacca and Pantelleria. Amongst the first to notice it were the inhabitants of Sciacca, who were rightly worried by the column of smoke rising from the sea's horizon and by the earthquake tremors which rumbled ominously from the beginning of the summer of that year. By August the islet had reached its maximum size: about three miles in circumference and about 180 feet high. It had been an object of not entirely disinterested curiosity on the part of several nations and had been given various names: Sciacca Island by the Sicilians, Ferdinandea by the Bourbons (in honour of King Ferdinand II), Julia by the French (because it had emerged in July), Graham Island by the British (after a politician of the time). And the British, the French and the Bourbons instantly declared it as their own national territory, sending out ships to hoist their flags. The diplomatic and military wrangle which it caused did not last long. The solution came directly from the island of Ferdinandea itself, which disappeared almost as suddenly as it had emerged, in the space of a few months, eaten away by the sea and the wind. It resurfaced briefly in 1863, and then was swallowed up once more. What survives of it today is an underwater volcano, whose summit reaches to just a few metres below sea-level, in a shallow stretch of sea called Graham's Bank.

9

At the edge of the town, just before the beach, you find two old stone-built basins, each one about ten metres wide and ten metres long. They are shallow and separated from the sea by a low, dilapidated wall. When it is high tide, the sea comes in through various breaches in the wall. Nowadays the basins are populated by thousands of crabs, but they used to contain turtles. These are the old 'turtle ponds'. Built in the first half of the nineteenth century, the turtles captured on the beaches were kept here, before being slaughtered or sold alive to the ships which stopped by Ascension.

The little museum at Fort Hayes, near Georgetown, holds Simon Frazer's diary along with some old photographs of that period. One of these shows the beach beside the turtle ponds with dozens of upturned turtles, their heads back and their paws stretched out to their full length, as if crucified. It is not easy to immobilize a turtle: in fact, it is almost impossible. The only way is indeed to turn it upside down. At that point the turtle stops resisting.

Around 1850 Simon Frazer was the commander of the Royal Marines on duty on Ascension Island. During the turtles' nesting period, which runs from January to June, he would recruit from amongst the Marines volunteers to patrol the beaches. Chosen from amongst the strongest and fittest, they would patrol in pairs, the luckiest being sent to Long Beach and Dead Man's Beach. The others ended up in English Bay,

South East Bay and North East Bay, which were far away and difficult to reach. It was not exactly a pleasant existence. Food supplies would arrive twice a week; all they had was a hut in which to escape the sun (there was not even a single tree) and to sleep; they worked by night, when the turtles advanced up the beach. The job was simple: to patrol the beach all night and, once a turtle was spotted, wait until she had laid her eggs before turning her over with the aid of sticks, and leave her there until, two or three days later, other Marines would come to load them up and transport them to the turtle ponds. At their peak the turtle ponds contained up to 300 turtles. And in any one season up to a thousand would be captured. Nowadays the number of turtles that arrive every year is between two and three thousand.

Even before becoming a delicacy for the tables of the aristocrats and plutocrats of half of Europe (most famously as turtle soup), and right from the earliest great voyages across the oceans, sea turtles had been a simple and efficient means of providing food that was easy to conserve for the crews of sailing ships. They were plentiful, they were easy to catch, their flesh was edible, and they could be kept alive for several weeks in a confined space without many requirements: overturned and flat on their backs as in the old yellowing photograph in the little museum on Ascension. That was why the sailing ships of the last century called in here: in the season of busiest traffic there would be up to five or six ships a week.

The sand at Long Beach has a golden, ochre colour. Other beaches have different colours: lighter, almost white sand, as on Pan Am Beach (the beach beside the airport built by the Americans was renamed thus during the war); or darker, almost black sand thanks to the presence of pulverized lava, as at North East Bay, on the other side of the island. Apparently there is another beach, called Crystal Bay, which has green sand, thanks to the presence of a particular greenish mineral called olivine, but it cannot be reached on land and is difficult to get to even by sea.

It is on these beaches that the turtles come to nest every year, and perhaps the colour of the sand contains some significance for them. In fact the colour of the sand influences the amount of heat that is absorbed from the sun's rays, and consequently also the temperature of the sand, which in turn, strangely enough, determines the sex of the baby turtles. As in other reptiles, the sex of the young depends on the temperature at incubation: just a few degrees difference, and the whole batch will be either male or female. This phenomenon was discovered in crocodiles when they started to be farmed industrially for their skins.

Graeme has brought some temperature gauges which we will bury on the various beaches. These are for the secondary aim of our journey to Ascension. They are objects about the size of a cigarette packet and they record the temperature every six hours for a whole year on a little solid electronic memory-cell: in a year he will come back here and if he is lucky, and the tides have not completely reconfigured the beaches, he will find his gauges and will be able to reconstruct the sand's temperature during the incubation of the eggs. This way he will be able to determine whether the sex of the young turtles really does depend on the colour of the sand.

I O

The only book about Ascension Island, *Ascension: The Story of a South-Atlantic Island*, was written in 1973 by an English journalist, Duff Hart-Davis. I managed to find a copy of it, some months after my return, in the San Francisco city library. It quotes a description by a sailor shipwrecked there in the seventeenth century: 'Any body would have believed that the Devil himself had moved his quarters and was coming to keep Hell on Ascension.'

On this island, described by a nineteenth-century traveller as a 'hell with the fire put out', the devil is very much at home. At least five places mention him: the Devil's Riding School, the Devil's Ashpit, the Devil's Cauldron, the Devil's Inkpot and the Devil's Punchbowl. Not bad for an island about a third the size of Elba.

A state of mind which was often to take hold of us in the early days, only to vanish again unnoticed, is the sense of disorientation and anxiety that this place evokes. My God, where have we ended up!

Every word we use summons up a primary meaning and a series of associations. Take the word 'hill'. How can Cross Hill be called a 'hill'? It does not work, the word evokes other associations (Pavese's Langhe hills, Hemingway's *Green Hills of Africa* . . .), which are not remotely like the lonely outcrop that towers over Georgetown. The slope is too steep and uniform, its surface too bare of vegetation, its colour too garishly red for it to be a hill. You would expect to find other similar 'hills' near by, but there are none. There are some, however, at some distance, erratically distributed throughout the island, some in clusters, others on their own, many with the edge of their crater still clearly visible.

Some days after my return from the island, driving along in my car, it suddenly struck me. The shape of Cross Hill and of many other volcanoes was an enlarged version of the mounds of gravel that a lorry has just unloaded: they have the same steepness and regularity, something totally unlikely in a natural mountain. They are like outcrops that have just been created and on which the forces that shape our environment have had too little time or scope to operate.

I have been on Lavezzi Island, near Corsica. It is constantly battered by the wind, which along with the sea has produced highly polished rock-faces, in bizarre, fantastic but very beautiful shapes. Why are these rock-faces 'very beautiful' and those of Ascension disturbing?

I think the answer is because *we sense that most landscapes have some meaning*. Through the workings of the wind and the sea they have received a particular configuration. Like the pebbles in the river, which can even be of different sizes and shapes, but which are all in some sense the same. Even in their variety one intuits that behind them there is a force to which the matter is subject, an order to which it has submitted, a pattern, a rule, a 'sense' ('almost an intention', as Brother Juniper would have said in Thornton Wilder's *The Bridge of San Luis Rey*, though he ended up on the funeral pyre for it). And on such elements we orientate ourselves or at least enjoy the illusion of orientating ourselves.

Elsewhere it is life which is the force that shapes and has shaped the landscape: bacteria, plants and animals have contributed in a variety of ways and through the most extraordinary adjustments to the most incredible outcomes. In both the microcosm and the macrocosm life has imposed its own forms. From the equatorial forest to the dried leaves gathered by the wind at street corners in autumn: everywhere we intuit the repetition of models, the presence of rules.

Lastly, man has with his civilization and technology imposed a further order: any urban, industrial or rural landscape is an example of this.

And wherever we sense an order (or more than one order) in the environment, there exists the possibility of orienting ourselves, of making predictions, of exercising some control, of using our own ability to combine different bits of evidence: of using our own 'intelligence'. Where all this is lacking, the upper hand is taken by the unpredictable, the disturbing, the nightmarish, the monstrous. Like a tree which suddenly sprouts an arm along with its boughs.

Ascension Island lacks the effects, or they are reduced to the minimum, of the three main *weak* – but ever-present – forces which have tamed our environment, making it in our view ordered, habitual and therefore beautiful: meteorology, biology and technology. Here one notices in all their power and impenetrability the unaltered traces of the enormous forces which are rooted in the bowels of the earth. Here dominates the threatening imprint of *strong* geological forces, explosive and primordial. The mouths of its forty volcanoes, their shape, size and distribution are unpredictable, chaotic, devoid of any sort of order. And so too are the rocks and stones which the cooled lava has become. How can control be exercised in such a world?

This is the source of the bewilderment which seized us on our arrival and of the nagging sense of unease which continues to pervade us throughout the early days. And yet, gradually, the astonishment and anxiety will dwindle until they disappear, thereby proving the almost limitless capacity we possess to adapt and make ourselves at home in every type of external environment.

High above the beach next to the turtle ponds a huge black bird wheels in the sky. Its colour, its forked tail and those large thin wings, initially curved forwards and then backwards, all make you think of a pterodactyl, one of those flying dinosaurs that we have all seen in children's books. It is a frigate-bird surveying the beach from on high in search of young turtles. Its dark outline against the sky seems to blend perfectly with the surrounding volcanic landscape, thus giving it a further, disturbing touch of prehistoric magic.

II

Discovered by Columbus on 11 November 1493, on his second voyage, the island of Montserrat had taken its name from the monastery on the slopes of the mountains near Barcelona, the place whence a few years later Ignatius of Loyola would set out on his tortuous and painful mystic journey which would lead to the foundation of the Jesuits. Montserrat – the island – is one of the Leeward Islands of the Lesser Antilles, another remnant of the British Empire. In the seventeenth century Irish settlers established a colony there and from 1871 it became a British possession. It is a volcanic island. But the volcano had never shown any signs of life since Columbus discovered it. Newspapers called it 'an emerald isle': famous rock groups recorded there and several celebrities built their homes on it. A few years ago, Soufrière Hill burst into life. In the last months of 1997 came the news that two thirds of the island had been destroyed, buried under lava. Or, to be more precise, under 'pyroclastic flows', which are much more dangerous than lava: these are 'clouds of fire' made up of gases, vapours and burning ash which the volcano emits and which, being much denser than air, rush down its slopes destroying everything in the way. The vast majority of the 13,000 inhabitants were evacuated, and probably forced to leave the island for good.

Could the same thing happen on Ascension, an island which from the time of its discovery onwards has never been known

47

to have had an eruption? The time elapsed since then has been too short, and the evidence on the island is unambiguous: the last major eruption took place five or six hundred years ago. When the Portuguese discovered it, the lava had, so to speak, just cooled.

The day when one of Ascension's volcanoes becomes active again and threatens its survival, there will be one difference compared to Montserrat. There will be no families forced to abandon houses where they have lived for generations and where they thought their own descendants would continue to live. For the fact is that people do not live on Ascension for generations. There is not and never has been a resident population. Nobody has stayed here for more than a few years.

Everyone is just passing through. Graeme came down here five years ago for three months. He got to know lots of people: when he came back only two of them were still around. Twenty years ago the Falklands War, albeit only indirectly, hit the life of the island like a cyclone, turning it overnight into the strategic base for all the British war operations. Since then life has never been the same here. For a few weeks the airport became literally the busiest runway in the world. From that point on the airport was resurrected, a new village was set up for the RAF pilots, the hospital was revamped, and, most important of all, a twice-weekly flight from Britain was established. Today there are only about ten people who were on the island before the Falklands War. And none of them remembers the Second World War, when the Americans arrived and changed the nature of the island even more dramatically.

One of the few people to remember the 'pre-Falklands' period was the dentist's nurse. I had gone to find John, not because I was suffering from toothache, but because he and his fawn-coloured dog were amongst the nicest and most biddable creatures I had met. He had told me that he still kept a photocopy of an article from the *National Geographic* magazine from 1946, which dealt with Ascension – curiously, from that time onwards, that magazine, though always on the lookout for unusual places and landscapes, had never bothered about the island again.

Instead of the dentist I found his nurse. She was a woman around fifty, very kind, with a rather languid way of talking, or rather drawling. She too was from Saint Helena and she would go back there in a few years' time. Her skin was the colour of milky coffee, her eyes were blue and smiling; she was still very attractive, a beauty that had faded somewhat but which allowed you to guess how irresistible she must have been when young. I went back several times to the dentist's surgery. He did not have a lot of work: he was meant to be in the surgery every afternoon from 2 p.m. onwards, but he had very few appointments and they never started before 4 p.m. My friends bad-mouthed me, saying I went there for ulterior motives. In fact my only desire was to hear the stories of one of the few people who still retained some memory of the island's history.

I would come back to my room and transcribe her stories into my notebook, which stupidly I would later lose. In it I wrote my impressions of the entire course of the journey right down to the last stretch, the flight from London back to Italy. It was then, just as we landed, that I placed it – I have a clear memory of it – in the pocket in front of my seat, and that was where I left it. Who can say how accidental that loss was; it seems as though I had felt the unconscious need to get rid of it just as I got back home. To exercise a kind of censorship. Perhaps what I am writing now is an attempt to fight back against our unconscious yielding to the omnipotent 'reality principle'.

So I have to work from memory: what remains is the imprecise record of a life lived between Ascension and Saint Helena. Only once had that woman been abroad, to visit her relatives in Britain, a country which she had found beautiful but too expensive, frenetic and cold. On Ascension she earned enough, but Ascension was not much good either. Like everyone else, after the many years spent far from Saint Helena, she felt homesick for her island: it was greener, calmer, more normal. She was counting on going back there for good next year. With her savings she would buy a house in which she and her husband could spend their old age. Although hers was a modest salary by European standards, it was much better than any-thing she could have earned on Saint Helena, where there is no work and people live on subsidies. Her daughter would stay on Ascension because she had studied – they had sent her to Britain for that – and had found a job at the BBC before she was even twenty-six. After that age the children of those who work on Ascension have just two choices: either they have found a job or they have to leave. There are no exceptions.

The nurse spoke about the period before the Falklands War, when the British seemed to have forgotten about the island, and the South Africans still had their telephone receiver and transmitter station on it and the Americans were more numer-ous than they are now. There were very many people from NASA. Several aeroplanes would arrive from the USA, but they were all military planes. Once a month the ship from Britain would come, heading for Saint Helena and Cape Town, or on its way back. For civilians there were four or five charter flights a year. My friend the nurse remembers: yes, she recalls there was a flight in autumn, because the children would leave to start school, and another flight around Christmas, perhaps also one in springtime . . .

Another person who knew the island from way back was the barman at the Exiles' Club, the British bar. He was very black, with a surly, scornful look. He reminded me of Quarrel, the black fisherman who was initially James Bond's enemy and then became his friend in the first film, *Dr No*. The barman was also from Saint Helena, but unlike the nurse who had only done that one job all her life, he had done thousands of jobs. As a young boy he had helped an American expedition to replenish the turtle population, and would go and collect their eggs on the beach. He had initially been in the employ of the British, then the Americans, then the British again. He had also gone to work in the USA. He had been a barman for five years. He looked worldly wise. But it was impossible to get him to tell you anything. Partly because of his impenetrable accent, but particularly because the minute he realized that what he was saying was of any interest to the listener, he immediately clammed up and changed the subject.

12

The comparison with the moon comes back to me: when man eventually goes regularly to the moon, for a long time nobody will want to settle there definitively, or colonize it. The people there will be on a mission, for the limited time stipulated in the employment contract, impatient to get back home.

Exactly as on Ascension. There is no private ownership of the land. There are only employees who work for the four or five companies which own the island; which 'use' it. Explicitly and with no frills, with typical Anglo-Saxon bluntness, the group of companies which own the island is called 'The London Users' Committee': these are Cable & Wireless (the telecommunications firm), the BBC, the CSO (the Composite Signals Organization is a semi-clandestine British government agency, dedicated to listening to the airwaves), the RAF and the Americans.*

There are no farmers, fishermen or shopkeepers, nor any private property or initiative. There are not even any taxes. The supermarket and the other small shops in Georgetown, Two Boats Village and Travellers Hill belong to a single agency, the AIS (Ascension Island Services), an offshoot of the companies that own Ascension. The AIS sees to the 'running'

---

* This reflects the situation as it was in 1997. The official status of Ascension and its inhabitants is likely to change in the near future. See references in the Webography.

of the island, from the harbour to the shops, the streets, the food supplies and the health service. Clearly it is not quite true that there is no private initiative.

It is Sunday morning and there is an unusual amount of activity on the jetty. There are three or four cars and a couple of vans parked there as well as half a dozen onlookers staring out at the sea, which is as grey as the cloud-covered sky. The little trawler – more like a biggish launch – has been out all night and has just moored off the coast. A small fishing smack has gone out to it and is now returning. All around, the usual fantastic whirling of the booby birds in the wind.

From above the jetty I watch the fishing smack arrive. On board are Saint Helenians who had been fishermen on their own island and who can do their old job here only on weekends or when their work-shifts allow them. I count seven men and a young lad who holds the tiller: they are all black, but each of different gradations of black. Two are standing at the prow, the others are sitting on the sides of the fishing smack, whose bottom is full of fish. I manage to make out sixteen big fish, either tuna fish or others which I don't recognize. Once the boat is moored, each fisherman grabs two fish by their tails and drags them up the landing steps and along to where the jetty begins. Here there is a kind of cement counter under which they drop them. As they pass me by, I notice that the tuna's dorsal fin is bright yellow, canary colour. Just like – I will remember later – the description in one TV commercial that seemed to be everywhere for a short time. Opinions, comments and witticisms all fly about: the fishing has gone well – I gather – though not exactly wonderfully well. Out of a car pops a box of cans of beer, which they all help themselves to; I too am invited to join in, but this is too early an hour for my tastes.

Two fishermen, wearing huge green aprons and wielding big knives, get ready to slice and gut the fish. They quickly cut into the skin and skilfully separate it from the flesh, which in the tuna is red just like that of a mammal. A second boat arrives with another twenty or so tuna fish and then a third with an enormous tuna: it has to be tied with a rope and it needs six men to haul it up the pier. This huge tuna is hung head down on a support in order to weigh it. This sparks off fierce discussions about whether the scales are accurate: the question is whether this tuna is heavier than the one last week, which holds the record for the year. The poor fish is hauled up and then down again, the scales are checked several times; in the end the fisherman and his mates who caught it reluctantly have to admit defeat: it was close but the record is still intact.

The number of fish-carvers increases. There are now about ten of them around the counter. The noise and good humour have reached a peak. The tuna remains are thrown back into the sea, which immediately just swarms with blackfish, which are absolutely voracious but inedible. Everything that is thrown in hardly has time to touch the water before it is gobbled up in a foaming whirlpool on which the thousands of fish converge. When the agitation dies down, there is no longer any visible trace of the carcass thrown into the sea.

The fishermen at work at the counter are almost as fast at their work as the blackfish swarming in the sea underneath them. The meat is divided up and allocated to each fisherman. Soon each of them goes off happily carrying several plastic bags full of tuna, all destined for their own consumption and for individual, semi-clandestine trafficking. In just a few minutes the jetty is empty.

In many of the bigger, more attractive European cities, popular or tourist legends have it that a ritual act carried out in certain places guarantees, or at least increases the probability, that you will return to that city. A typical example: if you toss a coin over your shoulder into a fountain, you will return once more in your life to that place. And the tourists carry out the ritual.

On Ascension, however, there is a spot, near Georgetown, on the road that leads to Two Boats, where the opposite rule applies. There is a boundary stone, a kind of large kerbstone, coloured in a thousand different shades. The legend says: as you leave the island, in order to be sure of never having to return there, you have to go down there and throw some paint at the kerbstone. This is the only way to protect yourself from the risk of being forced to set foot again on that damned island. But – the legend continues – you have to do it secretly, by night, so that no one sees you; for if someone catches you doing it, your destiny will be sealed for ever and you will never be able to leave the island.

These are things that belong to the past, when Georgetown was called the Garrison, when the only inhabitants of the island were a few dozen sailors with their officers and a few black workers dragged over from Africa. Since then many things have changed. But some rules still hold sway. There are no true residents on the island. People only pass through Ascension. People live there because they work there, but they are destined, even forced, despite the fearsome legend, to leave sooner or later.

Several times we met people curious to know who we were: particularly in a place where everyone knows everyone else. The question was always: 'Who do you work for?', not 'Who are you? Where do you come from? What are you doing here?' The employer is the important defining element.

There is no memory of history and there are no old people.

13

A week has now gone by since our arrival. The work is under way. We've checked to see whether the satellite radio-transmitters are working. Every evening we've gone down to the shore at Long Beach.

Night falls suddenly, as it does everywhere in the tropics. We eat dinner early, at the Saints' Mess. When we leave, around seven, the sun has just set, and in the short time it takes to get to the Islander Hostel on the other side of the street, to nip into our rooms and come back out on to the veranda, it is already dark. In a matter of days we have established the routine that we will stick to throughout the month. In the kitchen we keep some good South African wine which we can buy at the supermarket. Floriano uncorks it while I set out the chessboard, Paolo gets out his book (Melville's *Moby Dick*), and Graeme turns the radio on to listen to the BBC news.

Floriano and I are little better than average chess-players, and, as he says, the winner is always the one who makes the second to last mistake. We spend several hours in this way with long periods of silence, punctuated every so often by crude insults, a rather exaggerated way of expressing disappointment at some mistake or of rubbing salt in the wound after some winning move: not exactly the ideal of chess sportsmanship. Outside it is pitch black: from the only social venue in the place, the Saints' Club, wafts every so often the sound of a juke-box or the voices of young people.

It is now ten o'clock: we start to go into action. The bottle has been finished for some time, two or three chess games have been concluded, and Paolo and Graeme are ready to move. Work now begins. We fill our bags with a change of clothes, glues, solvents, gloves, the satellite radio-transmitter, the radio receiver, night viewers, lamps – some we wear on our heads like pot-holers, others we carry in our hands – and everything else we need. We check that everything is in, we divide the weight amongst us and set off on foot.

We leave on our left the Saints' Club, whose music will stay with us for a bit, and on the right, the police station. At its door a policeman in uniform waves to us. On the same side is the Administrator's Office, empty and dark, and, a little further on, a little house also totally dark, surrounded by a low fence, with a closed gate beside which is a notice: 'HM Prison'. The last time there was an inmate was three years ago, the Administrator will inform us later. Two young men had come in a yacht from South Africa: they had hashish on board. They spent two days in prison, then they were expelled from the island, or rather – if you prefer – they were released. But not before they had paid a fine: the cost of their board and lodging during their enforced confinement.

The road winds down gently, first twisting to the left then to the right. After the policeman we meet no other people. We are at the bottom, at the last yellow streetlamp, where the tarmac ends. By now we are near the sea and we can hear its roar quite clearly. We go along the dirt road in the dark, parallel to the beach. After a few minutes I look up at the sky: this, I have discovered, is the best point to take in the awe-inspiring numbers of stars. Not before, when your eye is too accustomed to the light, but not much later either, when your eyesight has become totally adjusted to the darkness, and less able to appreciate the finer details.

We walk about a hundred metres. On our left is the beach, on the right the scrub. It is like the African bush, according to Floriano and Paolo, who have been there. This area was once called Benin City, and it was the headquarters of the Kru workers who were brought over from Nigeria by the British.

We leave the road and turn on to the beach shrouded in darkness. Immediately walking becomes a real effort: the sand is nothing but an uninterrupted sequence of holes left by the turtles. However, Graeme, who is almost maniacal about not disturbing the turtles that are probably around us, makes us keep our torches off. About halfway down the beach we halt and make a sort of base camp where we will leave our bags. In the dark we try to identify a landmark so we can find them again: the dark shape of a piece of tyre washed in by the tide and which has remained close to the water's edge. We are about halfway along the beach lengthwise, so two of us will go in one direction and two of us in the other, looking for a turtle.

I set off with Graeme along the shore as my eyesight gets used to the darkness. The moon has not yet risen, but there are no clouds and the landscape around the turtles' beach, faintly illuminated by the stars, is astonishing. On the right-hand side of the road, looking back, next to the town rises the dark outline of Cross Hill, while further on the vista opens out and in the distance looms the ghostly shadow of Green Mountain, the highest mountain on the island. Near its summit are two points of light: the Administrator's residence and the farm. Beyond that again, I can just make out the faint outline of other volcanoes, then, close to the sea, there is the only other point of light. This is Pyramid Point, at the far end of the bay: illuminated by huge lights, there rises in the distance against the darkness of the night the white, spherical outline – known as the 'golfball' – of one of the many tracking stations on the island. (Is it a radar system? Or an aerial? It is always lit up and every so often another mysterious blue or red flashing light appears near by.) Behind us the town is now asleep, while over the sea brood the dark shadows of the few boats that are anchored offshore. A bit further out are the lights of the petrol-tanker, a constant and somehow reassuring presence. Rising above the rhythmic roar of the breakers we hear periodically the noise of a cricket or the braying of a donkey.

Graeme and I walk along the water's edge, looking to see if any turtles have already arrived (you can tell by the tracks they leave on the sand), but ready to jump back when any heavy waves land. You have to be careful because in the darkness you cannot tell what the sea is like, and here the sea always has to be taken seriously. Once Floriano, walking along the shore in the daylight, was caught by surprise by a wave which knocked him over and almost dragged him out to sea.

We find some tracks: they have been made tonight and they are heading up the beach. We have now learned to distinguish fresh tracks from those of previous days, and to tell arrival tracks from departure ones. We follow them for a bit, then Graeme signals to me to get down and wait, while he stretches out and proceeds silently on his stomach along the sand and disappears into the darkness. He reappears a few minutes later to whisper to me that the turtle is immediately behind us: but there is still time, she has only just started to dig, and it will be at least half an hour before she starts laying her eggs. We are unsure whether to wait or to go looking for another one.

In the month spent on Ascension I saw many turtles. They arrive at night even in the worst seas: they start in January, when the enormous Atlantic rollers are still crashing on to the island. They emerge from the sea and slowly, with halting movements, start to climb up the beach: they drag themselves along sliding on their base (the flat lower part of their shell), pulling themselves forward with their powerful front paws

59

and pushing themselves with their rear ones. Behind they leave a broad track, like that of a caterpillar vehicle.

Their movements are as elegant in the water as they are clumsy on dry land. What we notice in other animals of terrestrial origin which have adapted themselves to an aquatic environment (seals, penguins, crocodiles, hippopotamuses) is noticeable also in the marine turtle.

Every minute or two they stop, perhaps for a rest. Then they stretch out their necks, waving their heads in various directions, as though to search around on the lookout for danger. In actual fact, Floriano explained to me, the marine turtle's eyesight is adapted to underwater vision; and just as we, who see perfectly well through the air, have blurred vision underwater (unless we wear a mask), so the turtle sees badly on land for the same reason, namely an unsuitable curvature of the fore part of the eye, the cornea. This, by the way, apparently rules out the possibility that the turtles in their long voyage to Ascension and back, orientate themselves by the stars, unlike many migrating birds which seem to do so. Here on land they explore the environment by other means: by sound and, above all, by smell. If they sense danger, they return to the sea: they will come back to lay their eggs later that same night or on one of the next nights.

Once she has climbed a small way up the beach, the turtle wanders around a bit until she finds a place to begin digging a hole. With her forepaws which, like the rear ones, have been turned into huge flippers, she carries out movements similar to those which she uses to swim, bringing both paws forward, sinking them into the sand and making them wheel sharply outwards and backwards with a brusque movement. At every such move, the sand is lifted up and flung back a distance of several metres. After every eight or ten thrusts, she stops, in order to rest, to check the area, and to take deep breaths. If you hear it up close, the sound she emits is terrifying: something between a panting gasp, a deep death-rattle and bestial breathing. Moving forward or sideways every so often, she gradually sinks into the hole making herself invisible in the night.

After finishing the main hole in about three quarters of an hour, the turtle stops moving, then after a long pause begins preparing a second, smaller hole, this time using her shorter hind paws. With great caution, using them alternately like little spades, she digs a cavity that is about 40–50 centimetres wide and deep, in which to lay her eggs.

Sometimes, during this preparation, the turtle notices something wrong, and interrupts the construction of the hole in order to move a bit further forward and start again from scratch. On several occasions, after finding a turtle and waiting patiently for her to begin laying, Graeme would come back from his reconnaissance and whisper to us: 'She has given up.' One night a turtle on to which we had attached the radio twelve days previously, and which had come back to build her nest (each turtle lays her eggs four or five times), emerged from the sea around 2.00 a.m., and laid her eggs only after three abortive attempts. That was why we then found her still on the beach when the sun rose, and were able to photograph and film her, thus getting our reward for a whole night without sleep.

After a while Graeme goes back to see the turtle, and decides that the time should be about right: as soon as she starts to lay, she will not be deterred by anything any more, obliged as she is to carry out to the very end her laborious series of programmed actions. We will thus be able to switch on the torches, get closer, stand around her and apply the radio-transmitter to her back without her offering the least resistance. Nothing in her behaviour will suggest that she takes any notice of our presence. I set off to tell the others and to collect the bags.

When we come back Graeme is already at work. He has crept up behind the turtle, as far as the hole in which she is laying her eggs, which he is now getting ready to measure. Each of us has our duty: Paolo and Floriano prepare the glues and the mastics, I keep the diary and transcribe the measurements that Graeme calls out to me. I join him and, with great caution, stretch out alongside him but a little bit behind: we have to be careful not to cause the collapse of the walls of the main hole, or even worse, of the hole for the eggs, which I can now see clearly with the lamp on my forehead. On the bottom of the turtle's huge body, there seems to be a kind of casket which is hidden by the small triangular tail and by the rear paws which Graeme has held apart with delicate gestures. Down there we can see the eggs: lit up by our torches, white and round and little bigger than ping-pong balls, they come down in clusters of three or four. By the end – but we will not measure all of them – she will have laid about a hundred eggs. Stretched out on his stomach, Graeme collects them, measures them with callipers, and then places them back with the others. He whispers: 'Forty-one point seven', 'Forty-two point one', 'Thirty-eight point nine' . . .

To keep the turtle still while the PTT is attached (this is the acronym for the satellite radio-transmitter, the Platform Transmitter Terminal) we had brought a special cage for the purpose. The 'mummy' was an ingenious object, light and easy to dismantle, transport and reassemble. It consisted of a wooden board, reinforced by aluminium, and lined on three sides by well-padded edges to prevent the turtle hurting itself. We only used our turtle-cage once, and no more. The idea was that the turtle would enter through the open side and get trapped in it, thus allowing us ample scope for the work we had to do. It was a complete disaster. Once the first turtle arrived in the cage, she went to the far end and overcame the barrier without any difficulty and started to come out the other side. A night to forget. There was no contest between us four struggling ungainfully to restrain her and the turtle who, possessing much greater strength, escaped from us every time.

Abandoning the idea of containing the turtle by force, we realized that the only way was to use guile: in order to attach the radio on to her we would have to use the period when she was motionless trying to cover her eggs.

While the others are preparing the mastic, I have the chance to examine her calmly. She is a huge, awesome creature. In the dark that black shell, over a metre in length and half a metre in width, is like that of an enormous insect, or of a giant – Kafkaesque – beetle. In actual fact, when it is suitably lit up, the shell (sorry, carapace) is olive green in colour, hence the name green turtle, and it appears to be divided into symmetrical scales, just like the small tortoises that we are more familiar with. However, unlike the latter, the turtle cannot retract its limbs or head, which seem to be covered in a pale grey-green skin, which is also divided into scales. The front and rear feet are webbed, but possess quite impressive claws. Its face is square and slightly pointy at the front; it has two wide circular nostrils above which are big round black eyes which sometimes look totally inexpressive and at others seem to give the creature an almost amiable look.

The process of attaching the radio-transmitters proceeds swiftly, under Paolo's orders, who in this phase is in charge of operations: under the light of our torches the top of the carapace is smoothed with sandpaper; a first layer of glue is applied, then the mastic with which we prepare a housing for the PTT. The PTT is then pressed on to the mastic, and long strips of glass wool are placed crisscross over the PTT and the area of carapace next to it, and the whole thing is made secure by brushing on a very sticky solvent. This is all a battle against time. Once she has finished laying her eggs, which she does in about a quarter of an hour, the turtle begins to cover the egg-cell. She does this with great care and precision, with slow movements of her rear legs that remind you of the movement of human hands kneading flour.

We have to try to finish before the turtle stops covering her eggs. As long as she is only moving her rear limbs there is no problem. But if one starts late, or if there are hitches, things become more complicated. Just like at the start, when she built the main hole, so now the turtle begins to fire sand behind her with powerful, broad, swimming motions of her front paws, in order to hide the place where she has laid her eggs. There are times when it is safer to stand clear of the range of her paws. If you get a whack on your leg, it can be sore, very sore, as we all found out sooner or later. In order to give the finishing touches, we have to wait for her moments of rest, when the creature pauses to emit her incredible sighs.

Even when everything seems done, we still have to wait. We have to prevent her from returning to the water too quickly: the glues and mastic have to dry. Sometimes there is no problem, all we have to do is to check the turtle every so often, as she is the one who lets time go by, taking an age to cover the place where she laid her eggs. But on other occasions, unpredictably, she finishes much earlier and sets off: she comes out of the hole and heads towards the sea. In that case we have to intervene. Despite all the work she has carried out, she is still more powerful than us and it is impossible to immobilize her. Once more we have to act with cunning. We have to try to disorientate her by lighting up the sand next to her head. In this way we manage to confuse and distract her for a while. But very soon she will get her proper bearings again, and then we will have to try to turn her away from the sea by exploiting her moments of rest, but we have to be careful every time not to let one of her paws land a blow in our faces. This happened once to Paolo and for a second I was afraid that the turtle had removed his nose.

I look at the clock: it is after 3 a.m. By now we can let her go. We do not bother her any more: she immediately heads in the right direction and drags herself towards the sea. It will take her another half an hour to get there. We could leave to get some sleep at this point, but we stay right to the end to follow her slow progress, halted every now and then by long pauses and loud breathing. In the mean time a slice of moon has risen behind the volcanoes and is bathing the beach in an unreal, silvery light. The turtle reaches the water's edge – she continues to move forward – a first wave washes over her, a second wave lifts her up gently and drags her sideways for a small stretch – she still continues forward – she reaches the point where the waves break, and is hit by one of the bigger waves; for a last second we can still see the top of her dark profile, illuminated by our torches against the white spray, and the radio aerial projecting from it, then she disappears completely into the dark sea.

We switch on the radio receiver and wait. After a few minutes the radio makes two brief, croaking sounds. Everything is all right: the turtle has surfaced in order to breathe, the radio has emerged briefly, the PTT has been activated and sent out its signals to the satellite. Everything is going as well as it could. It is four in the morning, we can all go off to sleep.

We will receive news about her in a few days, by fax from Floriano's institute: we will find out whether she has started out again on the way home. But where is her home?

14

The destiny of Ascension Island suddenly changed when Napoleon, after defeat at Waterloo, handed himself over to the British and was exiled to Saint Helena. That was when, in order to be quite certain of avoiding other reverses after his escape from Elba, the British decided to take Ascension Island.

Sir George Cockburn was the captain of the *Northumberland*, the ship that was taking Napoleon to Saint Helena, and it was to his safekeeping that the prisoner was entrusted; and he was also the person who decided off his own bat to occupy Ascension. Duff Hart-Davis tells us that Cockburn, a few days after arriving at Saint Helena with Napoleon, sent out on a special mission the *Zenobian* and the *Peruvian*, two vessels from the naval squadron that had arrived escorting the *Northumberland*. (The *Peruvian*, moreover, had already played an important role in the voyage to Saint Helena, transporting two hundred bottles of fine French wines to improve the Emperor's table.)

The instructions, in a sealed envelope to be opened only once the ship was on the high seas, were to proceed to Ascension. If the island turned out to be uninhabited, the captain of the *Peruvian* was to set foot on dry land, take possession of the island, hoist the British flag and leave a garrison there with an officer, ten soldiers, a cannon and whatever else was deemed necessary for its defence. If, on the other hand, they found ships of other nations off the island, they were to wait, keeping their intentions secret, until the other ships left. Lastly, the instructions concluded, if the island turned out, contrary to all expectation, to be occupied by another nation, they were not to interfere in any way, but to return immediately and bring back this news to Saint Helena.

Blown by favourable winds, the ships reached Ascension after five days' sailing. They found no one there. They ran up the British flag. That was how, as the logs of the two ships testify, at half past five on the afternoon of 22 October 1815, one week after the arrival of Napoleon on Saint Helena, Ascension Island became British without a single shot being fired. And still without a shot being fired, it has remained British to this day.

The story of Tristan da Cunha is similar. The British also sent a garrison down there – in 1816 – worried that the French (and in particular the Americans, whom they feared even more) could use the island as a base from which to launch a coup to free Napoleon. But unlike Ascension, they found it inhabited. Tristan is much further south, also beaten by the winds and exposed to Atlantic storms, but – and this is the crucial thing – it has water. They found a strange man on the island, called Tommaso Corri, an Italian from Livorno (his name was anglicized to Thomas Currie), who had gone there six years previously along with an American, one Jonathan Lambert. The latter had decided to declare the island his personal property, proclaiming himself Emperor of Tristan da Cunha. He had also taken the trouble to publish this news in the *Boston Gazette*. Then one day, in 1812, he had gone to sea to go fishing and had never come back. Just to make sure, however, the British made Corri sign a declaration recognizing the British primacy on the island. We shall return to Corri's or Currie's real character shortly (he remained on the island and died there in 1817).

When Napoleon died in 1821, Tristan lost all its importance

and the garrison was withdrawn. But a Scottish sailor, called William Glass, decided to stay on, along with his very young black wife, a twelve-year-old South African, who subsequently bore him sixteen children. As time passed other sailors or ship-wrecks arrived, amongst whom, in 1893, were two Italians, Andrea Repetto and Gaetano Lavarello, from Camogli, who had escaped shipwreck from the brig *Italia*. Even today a third of Tristan's three-hundred-strong population has their surnames. In 1962 a sudden volcanic eruption caught the only settlement, Edinburgh, unawares. The inhabitants had to take refuge on a nearby island and were then subsequently evacu-ated by a British warship. They were brought to Britain and placed in a refugee camp for some time. They were unhappy there, so were taken to a remote island in the north (maybe in the Orkneys or Shetland Islands), but they did not feel happy there either and, after two years, they went back to Tristan da Cunha.

But the most detailed historical source is *The Annals of Tristan da Cunha* by Arnaldo Faustini (another Italian!). Professor Arnaldo Faustini (that is how he is titled on the internet site where I found this information), born in Rome in 1872, had been quite a famous polar geography expert at the turn of the century and in 1915 had moved to the USA, where he worked at the American office of the Banca d'Italia. After his wife's death in 1990 (he had by then been dead many years), their daughter, going through her father's papers, found a manu-script that no one knew anything about: the aforementioned *Annals of Tristan da Cunha*. Which she then published on the internet.

It is a detailed chronicle of the island. From its discovery in the first months of 1506, when Tristão da Cuña's ship, off course in a storm, had first sighted the island; to the story of Lambert and Tommaso Corri, who it seems was in reality some kind of pirate who had killed his American companion;

to the terribly hard, remote way of life lived by a bunch of colonizers who had taken root on the island for more than a century ('1887: No ships called at Tristan during this year').

The Annals end on 23 March 1925 with the reply from the Minister for the Colonies to a London lawyer who had become the spokesman for the islanders' petition: 'The Secretary of State will lay before HM the King the expression of loyalty to his Majesty conveyed in the petition, and a letter will be sent to the islanders when an opportunity occurs. HM's Government have, of course, every sympathy with the desire of the petitioners to obtain an annual mail, and the question of the possibility of providing more regular and frequent communication with the island has recently been under careful consideration [. . .]. It is feared, however, that having regard to the considerable expense and other difficulties involved, the Lords of the Admiralty [. . .] cannot undertake to arrange for a yearly visit of one of HM's ships to the island [. . .]. Such a visit can be made every three or four years . . .'

15

It is two o'clock in the afternoon. The time when – according to Noël Coward – only mad dogs and Englishmen go out. The sun is ferociously hot overhead; but the heat is tempered a little by the tropical wind which, as ever, is blowing from the south-east. My friends are on the veranda, plotting on the map the position of the turtles, whose coordinates have just been faxed from Italy, and wondering what they are doing. I take the van to go for a drive.

It was not easy to find that van. Like everywhere else where there is no demand, there is no supply either: as there are no tourists, no one had got organized to hire cars. The Administrator had been quite clear about this right from our first meeting: 'I can't do anything about it,' he had said, 'I don't have a car I can give you for a month, and the firms that operate here all have their own, and they are pretty few anyway. I could maybe let you have the Catholic priest's car when he leaves in a fortnight. Or you could try one of the Saints. But you have to do it yourselves: if I ask, it will only make it more difficult.' And so, after a week, we found a Saint ready to hire out for cash his ramshackle van.

There is petrol in it and water too, which, according to our Saint's advice, needs to be topped up every day. I take to the road with the usual initial strain of readjustment – because here they drive on the left – and head south, towards the American military base and the airport. The road runs high above the coast, through a bare, inhospitable landscape of scrub. I only meet a couple of cars – as we pass we wave hello – and a group of donkeys advancing calmly one after the other along the side of the road. My driving by does not upset them, except for a baby donkey which in fright rushes to its mother and huddles close to her side.

I switch the radio on. It is tuned to the wavelength of the BBC's Africa Service. The programme, which is being broadcast from Ascension itself, from the giant aerials on English Bay, is a serious one, particularly for Africa: how to protect yourself from AIDS.

Two tall flagpoles flying the American and British flags mark the entrance to the base. On the ground are two old cannons, a plaque recording the building of the airport during the Second World War and the inevitable white mile-post, full of horizontal arrows pointing in every direction and giving the distance to a huge variety of places: so many miles to Los Angeles, so many to Singapore, and to many other places, including the North and South Poles. There is no perimeter fencing, but it is immediately clear that here you are entering a different world. On my radio a doctor is explaining the advantages of the condom.

I worked many years ago in an American base near where I live, and I have seen others in Germany, in the USA and at Okinawa in Japan. Everywhere you find the same style, the same kind of buildings, the same successful attempt to re-create the feel of a 'smart' suburb of a small town in the Midwest. No matter what lies beyond the base, the hills of Central Italy, the fields and woods of Germany, or the extinct volcanoes of a remote island in the middle of the ocean, you always find a grid of streets, huge cars, low houses surrounded by lawns, and then beyond this the depots with lorries, cranes, fork-lift trucks: everything is dark grey-green in colour, and to our eyes over the top in terms of number and size.

Just as entering Georgetown's Saints' Club in the evening

is the same as leaping thousands of miles north and being transported miraculously into the noisy gloom of a typical English pub, so here setting foot in the American Base's Volcano Club is a similarly miraculous journey, heading northwest for God knows how many thousands of miles and ending up in any American bar. It is just as noisy, but the noise is drowned by country music, and just as dark, but periodically lit up by shafts of pink and turquoise lights. But it is much bigger, more colourful, comfortable and brightly lit, and bristling with well-built young males and females of the most diverse ethnic origins, all chewing gum, mixed up here and there with older, paunchy would-be cowboys. Beer reigns supreme in the Saints' pub, and here in the Volcano Club it is also well represented but overshadowed by spirits (whisky) and soft drinks (Coca-Cola). The walls are covered with slightly ageing colour photographs of the recent past: rockets leaving Cape Canaveral, Ascension seen from a satellite and inevitably partly covered in clouds, autographed pictures of the crews of the lunar expeditions and smiling astronauts visiting the NASA base which has now been closed for eight years.

The road climbs running alongside other volcanic cones and reaches the centre of the island. The landscape changes. Dry, yellow grass appears, the number of bushes increases and a few trees can be seen. We are in the centre of the island, on Donkey Plain, where there are many wild sheep and, as its name suggests, donkeys. On the radio the programme has changed: 'This – is – London,' the voice of the announcer articulates with clipped emphasis: then comes the news. On the left, in the distance, beside a small black volcanic cone appear three aerials, like three enormous salad bowls turned up towards the sky; on the right, beside the road, there is another small white parabolic dish: this is the Satellite Earth Station of Cable & Wireless, built in 1967, and it sits beside an uninhabited hut which functions as a geomagnetic observatory.

I drive up a few miles, while my view widens as in a dream on to the entire south-western part of the island. Below me is the enormously long airport runway. We have been told that it is suitable for the emergency landing of a Space Shuttle, should it ever need to land in this corner of the world. Beyond the runway the eye stretches out over the central plain, which is all pitted with both small and big volcanic craters, the largest of which is the outline of Green Mountain, on the right. On the opposite side, to the south, an endless expanse of lava, and further on, the infinite ocean. While on the north side the dark colours of the earth here prevail – black, yellow ochre, the rust-red of the soil and the dark green which becomes more intense as you look up towards the mountain – to the south, even more desolately, it is a dazzling, stony white that domi- nates (from the bird droppings which cover the fields of lava), interrupted sharply, where it meets the coast, by the intense blue of the sea.

I reach a little pass and look out on to a completely different landscape. This transition is brusque and unexpected: sud- denly everything all around is green. I have crossed into the eastern, windward part of the island, the side exposed to the tropical wind which brings humidity to the land. This road was built by NASA to lead to its centre for the study of outer space and for the Apollo expeditions which first took man to the moon. For several miles I meet no one, there are no build- ings and not even any aerials. Only the odd wild sheep, and on the tarmac, every so often, the shattered remains of a giant crab.

The centre was built in 1965–6 and closed in 1989. The Apollo missions are over and outer space is studied somewhere else. Two badly tended palm trees on the side of the road mark the entrance. Grass is growing amidst the tarmac of the car park. There is a single, empty block. The walls are flaking, some of the windows are broken, the fittings are covered in rust, on the windows you can see the reverse of transfers stuck there ten to fifteen years ago. Of the two huge parabolic aerials which tracked live the descent of man on the moon, the only trace that remains is the enormous cement foundations in the ground. The aerials have been dismantled and taken elsewhere. The only visitors now are the few Boy Scouts on the island who sometimes come down here on a trip.

I have come back a couple of times to this part of the island and had a long and lonely walk, while Floriano and Paolo were chasing God knows what small insects on the ground. After leaving the main road, I went along a dirt track which led down towards Cricket Valley, and then further on to the Devil's Cauldron. There wasn't a soul. No sign of human beings, no sound of voices or cars, nothing but the incessant whine of the wind. And, all around, the woods which might initially remind you of Mediterranean scrub. But those plants were not Mediterranean (no bushes, small sweet-smelling leaves or berries . . .), but something else, even though they were just as low and dense: these had bigger, shinier leaves, and flowers that were too garish, and small lianas. This was a cross between house plants in a greenhouse that have gone wild and an equatorial forest in miniature. The ground too, however damp and covered in leaves, was too sterile: you just had to scratch the surface with a twig to realize how thin was that layer of humus. This environment, bizarre enough in itself, was made even more strange by its principal – and for a very long time sole – inhabitant. In other parts of the world that undergrowth would have been colonized by squirrels, grass-snakes or rabbits; down there live only the huge aggressive land-crabs with their strident yellow-orange colour (*Geocarcinus lagostoma* is its scientific name).

It is not difficult to find them. All you need to do is stop along the path and look into the undergrowth: after a few minutes a big orange crab appears. They immediately sense your presence and right from the start behave in a way that appears anything but apprehensive. They do not seem to have the slightest urge to escape or hide. The latter would not be easy, given the colour of their shell. Instead they stay quite still, and they seem to be observing you through their hostile little eyes that are barely hidden beneath their shell, and make an open and threatening show of their terrifying claws.

At one stage the whole island was inhabited by thousands of giant land-crabs. In the nineteenth century, when people tried to cultivate the higher, more fertile lands, they realized that they were a problem. Their habit of digging holes made it impossible to create gardens or cultivate fields. They were exterminated by the Royal Marines. Ten pairs of claws from ten dead land-crabs, duly delivered to headquarters, entitled you to a certain amount of rum. Traces of the statistics regarding crab-claws – or rum – have remained in some document or other that allowed Duff Hart-Davis to claim that between 1880 and 1888 no fewer than 335,535 land-crabs were destroyed.

In this remote and uninhabited part of the island you also meet another inhabitant, who is less ancient but more furtive: the cat. They are very small cats, thin and very fast: when you meet one, it watches you for a second from a distance, but the minute you try to approach it runs away.

16

At the sight of a marine turtle on the beach at night, one might at first think it was a huge insect, but the second thought would inevitably go to its not so distant but less fortunate relatives: the dinosaurs.

Turtles are genuine living fossils. Their appearance dates from over two hundred million years ago, when the first reptiles began to establish themselves on the lands that had just emerged. This was primarily due to two new abilities that fish and amphibians did not possess: that of producing eggs that could survive outside water, and that of providing itself with a skin so tough and impermeable as to protect the animal from drying up. In some primitive reptiles this characteristic would take on a particular line of development: the scales on its trunk would blend with one another and with underlying ribs, hardening and thickening and producing an actual shell which was rigid and extremely resistant. This was just one of the many variations continually produced by nature, but this innovation was to prove a winning formula.

Other reptiles, like dinosaurs, established themselves in countless different species, until they became the dominant land animals in the next geological era, the Mesozoic, which runs from 220 million to 65 million years ago, and which was suddenly brought to an end by a cataclysmic event, probably a meteorite striking the earth. After that the animals that established themselves were birds, perhaps the dinosaurs' real descendants, and mammals.

Amongst the reptiles, the dinosaurs died out, but other species survived, giving way subsequently to serpents and lizards. Crocodiles lived on and so did turtles, which are much more ancient than them, and they retained the same skeletal structure for millions of years. This proves that this particular solution (a very tough, even though heavy and cumbersome, outer shell) was in the end more useful than many others.

Like all animals that live in the sea or in fresh water and breathe air, marine turtles are 'secondary' inhabitants of water, descended as they are from more ancient land turtles, which at a certain point in evolution, who knows how many millions of years ago, returned to the sea. Apart from the capacity to breathe, they retained another habit that was too important to be allowed to be modified: reproduction. That is why the female turtles return to land to lay their eggs.

When she has finished laying and covering up her eggs, the mother turtle returns to the sea. Unlike her cousins, the crocodiles, she will take no further care of her young. After about fifty days, if the sand conditions have been right, if no high tides have played havoc with the beach and destroyed the nest, and if no predator has discovered it, the young will be born. All of them – or nearly all of them – will be of the same sex, as we discovered.

Ascension has had the good luck to become the turtle island because of the scarcity of predators: there are no dogs or monkeys which know how to dig in the sand looking for eggs. Also humans, who elsewhere, as in Malaysia, Mexico and Africa, know the value of turtle eggs (you can find them in the markets of those countries), here respect them – at least for now. However, there are other enemies.

Both the laying of the eggs and the emergence of the young

on to the surface of the beach take place at night. First one baby turtle (or 'hatchling'), then another, then in quick succession the whole family in the nest pops out on to the sand and races towards the sea. They have to be born all together because only by working in numbers can they generate sufficient strength to burrow up through the sand from its depths. In addition, once out in the air, these numbers increase the chances of survival, at least of some of them. No bigger than ten centimetres in size, they are perfect miniature turtles. Quite often, in the long nights spent on the beach, we were surprised by a sudden frenetic activity below us: dozens of baby turtles, which had just surfaced from a nest, instead of rushing headlong for the sea had been attracted by the light of our torches.

What happens to the young was cloaked in mystery for a long time. Turtle experts spoke of 'lost years', impossible for us to reconstruct. To tell the truth, for the vast majority, their fate has always been quite predictable: they ended up as prey for some fish or bird. Nowadays it is believed that the few lucky survivors who are destined to reach adulthood, once they get far off shore and have used up their last few drops of energy, get carried along in the majestic circular ocean currents – which, like giant invisible rivers, flow across the oceans – drifting, feeding on plankton, small fish and small jellyfish, and are carried in this way for years, for decades even.

At a particular point once they have reached a certain size, the green turtles (who knows how or why) leave the open sea and stay close to shore. They become stationary. According to marine biologists (who, like all specialists, have developed their own impenetrable, exclusive jargon), their habitat becomes 'benthic' not 'pelagic'. Their eating habits also change: they become herbivores, feeding on marine vegetation. Then after many years they set off again, to reproduce, miraculously able to find the place they were born at least fifteen to twenty years previously.

The ability to return to the place where one was born in order to give birth to one's own children (animal behaviourists talk of 'natal homing') is one of the most fascinating and mysterious aspects of the animal kingdom.

The proof that this happens with turtles as well was established only a few years ago, and it is indirect proof. It is based on the study of mitochondrial DNA, which every animal, including turtles, receives from its mother. This is a kind of female equivalent of one's surname, which every human being receives from the father and if male passes on to his sons. Studies carried out on young turtles captured in different parts of the world have shown that every beach has its own characteristic and limited genetic markers of mitochondrial DNA. Just as in country villages, the majority of people have the same four or five surnames, because for generations the families have never moved, or even if they have moved, in the end they have always come back to their place of birth, so the fact that on every beach the baby turtles have the same three or four 'mitochondrial surnames' can only indicate one of two things: either each of them stays confined all its life close to its own beach, or, even if they move far away, they then return to the same beach where they were born in order to reproduce. But we know that the first hypothesis is not true. That would seem to leave only the second one: namely, that each turtle, once it becomes adult, after a decade or two, is able to go back across the oceans and find that beach, or, in our case, that most far-flung and isolated little island, on which it was born so many years ago.

There is another, less well-known proof, but it has not been ratified by sufficient scientific papers, though it is more direct and perhaps more convincing. Floriano mentioned it to me and I have seen a video about it: it concerns the work of George Hughes, director of a nature reserve that overlooks the Indian Ocean, near Durban in South Africa. Several species of marine turtles nest on those beaches. For over thirty years this man, along with his research assistants, has been conducting the same experiment on the young turtles that are born on the beaches there. In the birth season, when every night hundreds of baby turtles emerge from the nest and race towards the sea, the young are captured, collected in plastic containers that soon swarm with them and, before being released, marked in quick succession by breaking the edge of the carapace in one or two places, always the same breaks each year, but different breaks from year to year. Well, it was discovered that a large number of the adult females who came – and still come – to nest on those beaches have one or two breaks on their carapace, the sign of that small injury inflicted on them at the moment of birth.

There remain three crucial questions: why, how and where they go back to.

The reason why natural selection has favoured the emergency of this particular behaviour – in other words, the advantage derived from returning to the place of one's birth in order to bring one's own progeny into the world – can, perhaps, be guessed. The fact that a certain individual is alive indicates that it has been able to survive until that moment. A banal concept, perhaps, but one which normally implies in nature that it has overcome an infinite series of trials, the first of which (and surely one of the most arduous) comes at the moment of birth, when every creature is defenceless. To have survived those initial dangers, however much good luck might have helped, certainly proved that that particular place where one was born represented a favourable environment. And it is for this reason that perhaps it suits the turtles, despite the effort of travelling incredible distances and facing dangers which at first sight seem insurmountable, to return to that very place as the site where their progeny in turn will face this same adventure.

It is more difficult to reply to the question 'how?'. It is well known that some birds can orientate themselves by the position of the sun and the stars and by following certain scents that are in the air. Salmon too seem to use the sense of smell when swimming back up river. This has been shown in countless experiments, one of which is quite simple: if there is a river up which salmon are swimming, and a number of them are caught and carried down river a certain distance, beyond the confluence with another stream, and then thrown back into the water, the fish will all return to the point at which you caught them. This proves that when they came to the confluence between the two streams, their choice was not accidental. If however the salmons' olfactory organs are damaged after capture, half of them will swim back up the 'right' stream, half of them up the 'wrong' one. This shows that the choice between the two streams was due to their sense of smell, which was able to distinguish between the different 'scents' of the water of the two streams.

But does what has been proven for a short water course, where the choice was relatively simple (right or left?), also hold true for the infinite expanses of the open sea? Was the salmon that swims thousands of miles to return to the river where it was born already following the same scent that will help it to decide which of two streams to choose when it swims up the river? What do salmon (or turtles) use to orientate themselves in the vastness of the oceans? Little or nothing is known about this. But a later chapter will deal with this and with the question of 'where?'

17

Although Ascension is probably one of the places on earth with the highest density of aerials, there is no local television station or radio-transmitter. There *is* a television channel but this just shows old TV films and there is a very powerful BBC transmitter (the Atlantic Relay Station), which broadcasts news and comment to two continents through the BBC World Service in half a dozen languages (English, French, Swahili, Hausa, Spanish, Portuguese), but nothing that deals with the local life of the island.

The one real source of information is a little newspaper, the *Islander*, which has come out every Friday since 1971, run by some industrious wife of an employee of the BBC (or of the RAF, or of Cable & Wireless).

At present – we are at issue number 1,330 – the paper consists of about thirty typed pages stapled together. You can tell that the computer has been introduced recently – the paper has been word-processed enthusiastically if not yet entirely professionally. It costs thirty pence (or fifty-five cents).

I rummage haphazardly through the issues I have brought home:

OPTICIAN'S VISIT

Reminder:

Mr Eric Burton will be returning to the island on his annual visit from September 29th to 14th October. Anyone wishing to make an appointment must contact [. . .]. Bookings must be made by 27th June. Please give the following details: name, organisation, d.o.b., Tel. no. and please state whether you are a new or returning patient i.e. if you have seen the optician before, here or on St Helena. This information is important to enable Mr Burton to find existing records. Those who do not make a booking for any reason will not be able to see the optician.

There will be no special concessions for anyone and it may not be possible to make new appointments for people who miss their appointments or are late. If you just wish for a change of frames please make this clear when booking your appointment. Jennifer Ross.

As I write at my desk, I glance at the calendar: it is 12 October. Another two days and then Mr Burton will not be seen on the island for another year. And whoever forgets to turn up or arrives late will have to go without glasses (or keep the previous year's ones). Will the strict rules announced so far in advance by the inflexible nurse Jennifer Ross have been respected?

I wonder if Jennifer Ross is the same stern nurse (blonde-ish hair, no longer in her prime) that I met when I went to the hospital. I bet she is.

The second day after our arrival, I went to visit the doctor on the island, in the hospital. My friends teased me: 'You were grumbling about how you couldn't wait to switch off and get away from it all – at least for a bit – but now that you've got the chance, what do you do? The minute you can, you go off to visit your counterpart on the island. You can't keep away from hospitals.' And they were right. The fact is that certain professions are all-absorbing, and it is not easy to leave them behind. *Semel abbas, semper abbas* runs an old Latin saying of the Church: once a priest, always a priest, you are marked for ever. It is exactly the same for doctors. And it is natural to seek out those who are like you.

The doctor had gone out, and would probably be back later: but what did I want, asked Jennifer Ross. Like all good nurses, she protected her doctor, who would be lost without her. I explained who I was and what I wanted. She looked at me suspiciously. Then she said to sit down: the doctor would be back in a quarter of an hour. I sat down for a while beside two other waiting patients. The seats were on a veranda overlooking a square of black gravel, from which one's gaze broadened out to the sea. After a few minutes my natural restlessness forced me to move (and my being a doctor authorized it): I could not stay there like an ordinary patient, I had the right to explore, and in any case I was not disturbing anyone. But I was wrong. The nurse brusquely brought me into line: I was to sit down and wait. I told her I would come back the next day and left.

PERCY'S LAST STAND

A chapter in Ascension Island's history came to an end on Monday afternoon when Percy Yon closed the pump for the last time. Percy arrived on Ascension on 9 November 1962, when he came to work at the American base. He worked there for three years and then went back to St Helena. In 1966 he got married and then returned to Ascension to work for Cable & Wireless. He also served in the Police Department for a short time before returning to C&W and then switched over to AIS for whom he has been manning the pump for the last 13 years. Percy's wife Doreen and daughter Deborah joined him here in 1971 when Deborah was four years old.

Percy and Doreen left Ascension on Wednesday's Tristar for a pre-retirement holiday in the UK, where they will stay in Portsmouth. This will be their first visit to the UK and we hope they have a wonderful time. They will be returning to Ascension in time to board the RMS on 19 June and set sail for St Helena and retirement.

Everyone knew Percy Yon and his petrol station. It was the only one on the island, and it had, like the few other shops on Ascension, a highly personal and unpredictable timetable. We happened to go there for petrol a few days before Percy left 'for an early retirement holiday in the UK'. The person we found was an angry and violent old man, who at our request for a receipt for the petrol refused it and gave us only a mouthful of abuse.

People explained to us that poor Percy was in fact in despair:

he was leaving (or being forced to leave) the place where he had lived for thirty-five years, and above all he was leaving (or being forced to leave) his daughter and grandchildren (half of his entire family).

The paper also offered news about crime levels:

POLICE STATISTICS

The Ascension Detachment of the St Helena Police has released its statistics for the period 1 January 1997 to 31 March 1997. During this period the Police received and dealt with 51 reports. This number is the same as in the corresponding period in 1996. There were eight criminal cases, four up on last year and four cases were heard in court as opposed to none in the same period in 1996. There were the same number (seven) Road Traffic Accidents, as last year but only fifteen Road Traffic Offences compared with thirty four in 1996.

Out of the total number of offences taken to court the following figures are included: Offences against the Theft Act 1968: one in 1996, four in 1997, [. . .]. The total number of ships, excluding Her Majesty's Ships, that called at Ascension during the period was fifteen, there were thirteen in the same period in 1996; of these, this year fourteen were yachts. There were nine yachts in the same period last year. Finally there are 867 privately owned motor vehicles, all classes, registered, of these 682 are licensed. There are 107 motor cycles registered, of these 52 are licensed.

There are also offers of work:

SITUATION VACANT
Newspaper Editor:

Applications are invited for the post of Editor, *Islander* newspaper, Ascension Island, which becomes vacant in mid-August. This interesting position involves approximately two full days' work each week, variable amounts of job satisfaction and occasional frustrations. Previous experience is not essential. An understanding partner and a sense of humour are a distinct advantage. Perks include an excuse to gatecrash weddings and the chance to meet, photograph, and eat, some really interesting, exceptionally big fish.

Such is the kudos associated with this prestigious appointment that no salary is offered, however an allowance of £10 per week may be claimed towards the cost of employing domestic help.

Interested persons are invited to place their applications in the *Islander* box in the entrance to the Administrator's Office and are requested to do so as soon as possible in order to allow the selection board sufficient time to process the anticipated deluge of correspondence.

Finally I quote from a long letter in which the Administrator's Office outlined the main events of that April:

FROM THE ADMINISTRATOR'S DESK

This Saturday is the Ascension Day Fair, which will be held at Two Boats. I hope as many of you as possible will support this event [...]. Some very antisocial rat-bags are breaking into the Challenger Outward Bound Centre. They are causing expensive damage and letting the weather in [...]. Some of you will have met Dr Graeme Hays of the University of Wales, Swansea, here for a month with three colleagues from the University of Pisa [...]. They plan to super-glue ten small radio transmitters to the backs of some adult female turtles and then track their progress by satellite back to Brazil – or wherever.

Another visitor, who will be here [...] will be Peter Campbell (he was here in November 1995 to advise on whether income tax should be introduced – it wasn't). [...] Dr Perch is arriving on 13 May with his beetles to let loose on the Mexican Thorn trees (I am assured that it will not harm any other plant). [...]

David Henry – of the Saint Helena Coffee Company who is interested in taking over the management of the farm was here in April. The Local Management Group is continuing discussions with him [...].

Speed-bumps will shortly be installed on the road into Georgetown from the Base (drivers are going much too fast and someone will be injured if something isn't done – so be warned).

18

When Napoleon died, Ascension was not abandoned. It had acquired a certain strategic importance as a support base for ships heading for the Orient and the Pacific: the Suez Canal would only be opened fifty years later, the Panama canal a century later. It was also important in the struggle against piracy and, most of all, against slave-merchants. In fact, by the beginning of the nineteenth century, the British, moved by humanitarian motives and perhaps also by political calculations, had decided that it was no longer lawful to rob Africa of her sons and drag them in chains to America.

Ascension had one great advantage and one great disadvantage: the advantage was the healthy climate, the drawback was the lack of water. Both are due to the fact that it hardly ever rains on the island.

Compared with the continents on the same latitude (whether Africa or South America), there was not the same oppressive humidity, malaria or other infectious tropical diseases. Ascension thus became a place where one could deposit sick sailors.

It still has this role today. When, two or three days after arriving on the island, I visited the doctor, in his small but well-run hospital, I found as the only patient alongside my friend, Jeremy the policeman, a sick Japanese sailor offloaded by a deep-sea fishing-boat which was in the area.

*

Comfortless Cove is reached by crossing a wild, savage expanse of lava and going past the white spherical cupola of Pyramid Point, the furthest point of the bay which we saw every night from the strand on Long Beach. A signpost, written by some wit, greets you: 'Welcome to the Moon.' On your left, just before you reach the sea there is the Bonetta cemetery. The *Bonetta* was one of the many ships which used to call in at Ascension in the first half of the nineteenth century. It was engaged in patrolling the African coastline in order to combat the traffic in slaves, and it arrived on 28 January 1838, but she was not allowed to stop at Georgetown: on board yellow fever was raging. She dropped anchor off Comfortless Cove: those who died on board were thrown into the sea, those who died on land were buried near the coast, and their names recorded to this day by the tombstones in the small cemetery.

A rule stated that the soldiers of the garrison could not come into contact with the ships in quarantine (the soldiers would leave the provisions up near Comfortless Cove, and when they left, the sailors from the ships would come along). However, several epidemics broke out in the garrison, the worst of which took place in that same year, 1838. Twenty-five out of the hundred or so men stationed on the island died, amongst them Captain William Bate, who for ten years had been the Commander of the garrison.

In the year 1829 I received instructions from the Admiralty to proceed to the Island of Ascension, to make a report and survey of the island previous to the adoption of certain measures recommended by the Commandant, Captain Bate, of the Royal Marines, which would have the effect (if sanctioned) of confirming the final establishment of the island as a permanent station.

That is how the *Notes on the Island of Ascension* begin, written by the Captain of the Royal Engineers, H. R. Brandreth. In his description of the geography and geology of the island,

Brandreth initially stresses its extraordinary remoteness. But then he concludes:

The dark and rugged beds of lava, the deep red colour of the hills, the wild and capricious forms of the mountains and precipices, and the prevailing apparent recent indications of volcanic action, impart to the aspect of the island a character of total sterility and desolation that does not really belong to it. It is important to notice this, as the impression made on the transient visitor is perhaps to the last degree unfavourable; while detailed examination of the features of the island is calculated in some degree to remove this impression.

In fact it just takes a rare storm, one of those hurricanes that visit the island every ten years or so, and in a few hours the island is drenched with as much water as it receives in all the other years. Then you can see the whole island (apart from the stretches of lava) suddenly turning green again, and getting covered, however briefly, with grass: the seeds of this grass, carried here from goodness knows where by the wind, sea and birds, having lain dormant in the ground for goodness knows how long.

19

Up until a few centuries ago, baby turtles were not in any great danger, if they had the good sense to be born at night. If, however, they made the mistake of coming out during daylight, their death was almost certain. Paolo tells me that he once witnessed a whole nestful emerge one evening on to the sand, while it was still light and had just stopped raining. Perhaps they had misinterpreted the lowering of the ground temperature, which had been caused by the rain, as being caused by nightfall. The baby turtles had been immediately spotted by the inevitable frigate-bird wheeling high over the strand. Despite all their frenetic attempts to rush towards the sea, Paolo says that few survived.

In the last few centuries baby turtles on Ascension have encountered an even more fearsome enemy, capable of stalking them even at night: cats. Originally there were no cats on the island: so how could they have got there? Man brought them, in order to defeat another scourge: the mice and rats brought by the ships. Rats are a torment on many remote islands: on Tristan da Cunha to this day there is an annual national holiday called Rat Day, dedicated to capturing rats.

Ascension Island's rats were studied by the young Charles Darwin, amongst others. He stopped at Ascension on his return journey from his voyage round the world on HMS *Beagle*; he was with Captain Robert Fitzroy, a man his own age, destined to become Governor of New Zealand, but who was eventually to commit suicide. Darwin had set sail with him, by chance almost, after two other young naturalists – who had been considered abler than him – had declined the invitation. He was incredibly young, only twenty-three, and he returned four years later. Even more incredibly, all his subsequent work was, on close examination, a reworking of everything he had observed on that first voyage.

His first book, *Journal of Researches into the Natural History & Geology of the Countries Visited during the Voyage of H.M.S. Beagle under the Command of Capt. Fitz Roy, R.N.*, also mentions Ascension, noting that 'of native animals rats and land-crabs swarm in numbers [on the island]'. And it goes on:

Whether the rat is really indigenous, may well be doubted; there are two varieties [. . .]; one is of a black colour, with fine glossy fur, and lives on the grassy summit, the other is brown-coloured and less glossy, with longer hairs, and lives near the settlement on the coast. Both these varieties are one-third smaller than the common black rat (*M. rattus*); and they differ from it both in the colour and character of their fur, but in no other essential respect. I can hardly doubt that these rats (like the common mouse, which has also run wild) have been imported, and, as at the Galapagos, have varied from the effect of the new conditions to which they have been exposed: hence the variety on the summit of the island differs from that on the coast.

The rats of Ascension Island, then, as well as the famous finches of the Galapagos Islands, gave the young Darwin pause for thought, and perhaps inspired him in writing *The Origin of Species*, the founding text of all modern biology.

The anti-rat campaigns have worked, and today the problem of the Ascension Island rats has been solved: in the course of a month I only saw a couple of mice, never a rat. What does remain is the problem of the cats which have gone wild and decimated the thousands of colonies of birds on the island. If there are still today plenty of birds around Ascension this is due to the fact that beside the main island there is another, smaller one, little more than a rock, Boatswain Bird Island, which is out of the cats' reach. Here and on the more inaccessible rock-faces of the main island all the birds that have always been here still nest in their thousands.

Only the exemplars of a kind of tern, which spend most of their time flying over the oceans, return in the mating period to the main island. They are also called 'wideawakes', an onomatopoeic name which imitates these birds' cry and gives Ascension its other name: Wideawake Island.

I have been on Wideawake Fairs, the wild expanses of lava near the airport, where a mass nesting of wideawakes had taken place, and it was a startling sight: on the ground, for hundreds of metres all around, scores of birds' skeletons and corpses in a more or less advanced state of decomposition, and eggs, an infinite quantity of eggs, all empty, victims of the cats.

In 1957 the British Ornithologists' Union organized a scientific expedition to Ascension, to study its birds. This led to a book, *Wideawake Island*, a copy of which I found in the island's little museum. According to its author, Bernard Stonehouse, in the course of every nesting, about 750,000 wideawakes settle on Wideawake Fairs, and a mere 10,000–20,000 of these fall prey to the cats.

How numerous these birds were in the past also emerges from Captain Brandreth's report, which tells us that in those times, in a single week 120,000 wideawake eggs could be collected. Considering that the human population was barely over a hundred people, for this apparently highly prized product supply far outstripped the possibility of consumption.

20

The other roads that leads from Georgetown to the centre of the island climbs up along Cross Hill, and leaving the town and the bay behind emerges on to the central plateau of Donkey Plain. On the left you meet the only petrol station – Percy Yon's – and a little further on, the multi-coloured kerbstone, whose colour is constantly touched up by British or American soldiers as they finish their tour of duty on Ascension. You then reach One Boat, which really ought to be called Half a Boat. Cut sideways and placed in a vertical position, with its prow towards the sky and the sawn off part on the ground, it offered shelter in the nineteenth century from the blazing, equatorial sun to the convoys which left Georgetown to climb up the mountain or on their way back. Going along the same road, after One Boat we come to Two Boats, where, as its name suggests, there are two vertical boats.

From One Boat the road going off to the left leads to Pyramid Point and English Bay. *En route* you find the only golf-course on Ascension. For a long time it was in the *Guinness Book of Records* as 'the worst golf-course on the whole planet'. It is not hard to see why: that dusty plain, devoid of grass or trees, scattered with sharp stones and thorny bushes, and surrounded by that disturbing lunar landscape, could not have had many rivals for that title.

Going left to Pyramid Point you find yourself in the middle of the most desolate expanses of black lava on the island, while behind you stands the incredible Sisters Peak, formed by two high volcanic outlines whose slopes are totally smooth. It was here, according to geologists, that the last volcanic eruption took place about 500 years ago. And here too the Americans, the legal owners of this part of the island, experimented, over twenty years ago, with the LEM, the Lunar Exploration Module or moon vehicle, before sending it to the moon. Apart from the bizarre forms assumed by the black solidified lava, the landscape is made even more unreal by the dozens of triangular aerials, which, running in parallel rows, like so many inverted tripods, open their arms upwards towards the sky and the satellites.

To the right the road for English Bay takes you to other aerials. You can already see them in the distance, but it is only as you get close that you realize how high they are. There are four of them, in terms of shape similar to normal pylons, but gigantic in size. Each is connected to the other by thousands of wires of varying height which crisscross the sky forming a complicated, unfathomable geometric web. This is the BBC Atlantic Relay Station, from which the BBC World Service broadcasts its programmes to Africa and South America: the channel through which London's radio-programmes reach the two major southern continents.

Further on, we find the electrical power station. Here is where the fuel from the *Maersk Ascension* comes and is burnt. This is where the electrical energy and desalinated sea water is produced for the whole island – except for the American zone, where they organize absolutely everything for themselves.

From One Boat, the main road leads to Two Boats, where most of the British live. Once upon a time this was the Old Mountain Road, the ancient mule-track linking the garrison with the mountain-top, the only cool, fertile spot, where there were a few gardens, the odd little cultivated field, some animals, a small farm, and the hospital.

From Two Boats you also find the road that takes you to

North East Bay, the most remote beach and bay you can get to by car. You go down towards the sea, at first through an unusually pleasant area, a little wood of evergreens which at first sight look like pines or firs. They are in fact casuarinas, a kind of tree found throughout the tropics and brought to Ascension back in the first half of the nineteenth century. A huge colony of canaries nests there; these too were imported in the nineteenth century from the Canary Islands.

After crossing through the wood of casuarinas, you are back in the familiar volcanic landscape. First there is Perfect Crater, which has the shape and proportions of an archetypal volcano, and in the distance two less perfect volcanic craters but with equally illuminating names: Hollow Tooth and Broken Tooth. The road leads to the European Space Agency station, the Ariane site: when the rockets of the Ariane missions leave from the base in French Guyana, from about the third to roughly the tenth minute of the launch, the missions are under the control of the Ascension Island station, then for the next few minutes under the mission control of a base in Kenya, then who knows.

Suddenly, high on the coastline a landscape of harsh and solitary beauty opens up: a long, dark beach, like an open amphitheatre, majestic, deserted, beaten by the incessant wind. Further on, like receding curtains in a theatre, more and more rock-faces, and behind them the black outlines of Broken Tooth and Hollow Tooth. In front of you and all around it is cobalt blue: down below is the more intense blue of the sea, flecked with the white of the stormy waves, higher up is the lighter blue of the sky, interrupted by the broad and irregular surfaces of the scurrying clouds.

21

In the experts' jargon, the reconstruction of animal migration via satellite is called satellite telemetry. It has been available now for some years and is being used more and more often by biologists dealing with this type of problem. The system used by most is run by a Franco-American company which uses two satellites orbiting 500 miles above the earth's poles. They rotate perpendicularly to the earth's rotating movement, periodically flying over the poles, and thanks to the earth's rotation they gradually cover the whole of the earth's surface.

In our case, it functioned like this: the PTT attached to the turtles would send out signals every time the turtles surfaced to breathe. If at that point just one of the satellites was flying over the area, the signals would be picked up and if they were adequate the turtle's position would be plotted and sent to the European base at Toulouse, which in turn would send this by email to Floriano's institute in Italy – to be faxed, finally, back to us on Ascension.

Consequently every two days we knew where all our turtles were. But my friends seemed perplexed. The problem was that the signals from the first transmitters which had been attached suggested that the turtles were still near by, around the island. They did not seem to show any desire to leave.

This lasted a few days. Then, suddenly, one turtle stopped sending signals. The next day it was two turtles that we had no information on. Bizarrely, one after the other, four of the five transmitters we had attached stopped working. Each new fax brought more bad news. Our perplexity turned into concern, and then into increasingly bad moods. We had taken on board the notion that the turtles might not want to leave immediately. It was well known that once they reached the nesting site, they laid their eggs not once but at least four or five times, at intervals of ten to twelve days, before setting off on their return journey.

Now the problem was much more serious: the radios had stopped transmitting. There was only one solution: to stop attaching transmitters to them and hope that they would come back to nest so we could see what had happened. If the transmitters turned out to be faulty, we would remove them from the carapace and take them back to Italy to return them to the manufacturers and ask for new ones that worked.

So began one of the busiest periods of our stay there: it was no longer a question of finding just one nesting turtle, and attaching a radio-transmitter to it, but patrolling the *entire* length of the beach, checking *all* the turtles that throughout the *whole* night came in to nest. And without any certainty that the ones who came back were the ones we were looking for: they could have already left, or they might return to a different beach.

We would go down to the beach around ten. Even though it was dark from eight, the turtles waited a few hours before landing, so that we had time for our chess games. We would go down in tee-shirt and shorts to the beach which was still hot from the day which had just ended. However, the night was long and the wind never stopped, and as the night passed, the temperature became cooler and cooler, and we gradually had to put on more and more clothes in a sequence which each of us had devised in our own personal manner. We had two walkie-talkies which never worked, and a night viewer which by contrast worked very well. This was a telescope which could increase the brightness of the image and which Floriano had persuaded a colleague of his in Rome to lend him. The British army had these viewers: they are attached to rifles and allow you to see in the night. All you need is the tiniest amount of light from the stars, never mind moonlight, in order to be able to explore the landscape which appears entirely bathed in a fluorescent green. Like those images of the night-time bombing of Baghdad which CNN broadcast to the whole world during the Gulf War.

As I survey the beach I find myself fantasizing, as children do, that the viewer really is mounted on a rifle (its screen has the grid you find in rifle-sights) and that I keep an enemy in my sights during the night. In the distance, at the other end of the beach, there are people, and every so often the luminous point of a torch lights up. Perhaps they are men from the RAF, who have come to see the turtles. I like spying in the dark without being seen, and following the mysterious movements of indistinct outlines. How many are there? What are they doing? Are they coming towards us? Shall I shoot?

The long waits on the beach at night form, together with exploratory trips, one of my best memories of the stay. Stretched out on the sand, between patrols, we stay gazing at the incredible equatorial sky, which resembles a carpet swarming with stars. Floriano has brought a book that gives their names and those of the constellations. Looking north, towards the sea, just above the horizon is the Great Bear, while the Little Bear and the pole star are invisible, below the line of the horizon. It is impossible for us not to remember Dante's Ulysses:

> All the stars of the southern pole
> Were visible at night, but our northern pole
> Was so low that it did not appear above the sea-horizon.
>
> (*Inferno*, 26. 127–9)

Could Ascension be the island 'dark in the distance' sighted by Ulysses after sailing beyond the Pillars of Hercules and travelling south for five months in the Atlantic?

To the south, above the black masses of the volcanoes, we see 'All the stars of the southern pole': the legendary and the real Southern Cross; the complicated pattern of the constellation of the Centaur, along with Rigil Kentaurus, which in Arabic means the Centaur's hoof, the Alpha Centauri, the star closest to our solar system. And on the right, just above the town, Canopus, which in terms of brightness is second only to Sirius; while on the left, in a stretch of sky almost devoid of other stars, the long, curving row of stars in the constellation of Scorpio.

The darkness. We were immersed in the night, wrapped in blackness, relying on the faint light of the moon – when there was one – or of the stars. This must have been what the regime of night was like for man up until a few decades or centuries ago. But nowadays the *real* darkness – not the darkness constantly penetrated by car headlights, nor the limited, restricted darkness around streetlamps – but real, total and complete darkness is no longer known to us, or if it is, it is at most a fleeting experience.

That sight depends on two types of photo-receptor cells in the retina, called 'cones' and 'rods', I had known since the second year of medicine. Just as I knew that one of them, the cones, works when the light is stronger and gives us distinct vision and lets us recognize colours, while the rods allow us to see when there is much less light, but they do not guarantee distinct vision or the ability to make out colours. All these things I had studied God knows how many years ago. But it was only now that I realized the real significance of the experience of nocturnal vision, or 'scotopic' vision, as the experts call it.

'Rod vision' is something quite unique, especially if pro-longed for several hours, as happened to us: a different way of seeing – and of living in – the world, and it is difficult to find words to describe it, so distant is it now from our common collective experience. Being plunged into an unreal world devoid of depths and colours. Enveloped into a world that is not grey (grey is a colour), but milky-white, composed of chiaroscuro, shadows, unsubstantial forms, and shapes with evanescent outlines, which seem to dissolve if you stare at them and which reappear the minute you look briefly away from them. This too can be explained by physiology. That darker outline which I seem to glimpse, is it an illusion, or is it the outline of the rocks at the end of the bay? And the other, slightly lighter shape, which I seem to make out against the dark backdrop of the volcanoes, is it that dump of material halfway along the beach or is it an illusion?

Ghosts, ogres, vampires, spectres, elves and countless other presences that popular legends and literature have filled the night with have their origin in 'rod vision'.

22

The nights went by without notable incident. Checking the usual dozen or so turtles to no avail, patrolling the length and breadth of the ghostly beach who knows how many times, the crashing of the waves, the noise of the crickets, and every now and again the threatening braying of one donkey squaring up to another. The gold dome of Pyramid Point in the distance, looking like an astronaut base, the lunar outlines of the volcanoes, the limitless sky sparkling with stars, and crossed by scudding clouds. Every so often a shooting star: I have never seen such extraordinary shooting stars as I did on Ascension. Some were incredibly bright, and one night in particular I remember one of amazing intensity: an incredible emerald green trail disappearing into the sea.

That night Graeme told me about an event which he had witnessed five years previously, when he had spent three months on Ascension. He had become friends with some people, British and American, who had explained in great detail what was about to happen. The Americans, who from the time of the Second World War have owned about a quarter of the island, every so often use the waters around it as a testing ground to gauge the precision of their inter-continental ballistic missiles. In fact Ascension was an integral part of what they called the Eastern Test Range. At the bottom of the sea, at a depth of around 1,000 metres and some miles off the island, were placed a series of underwater microphones, with which it is possible to track with great precision the points at which the missile warheads touch the water. This system, called MILS (Missile Impact Location System) has now been placed, after the end of the Cold War, at the service of the United Nations, to monitor nuclear disarmament.

Graeme had witnessed the preparatory procedures: in the afternoon he saw some balloons go up; night fell and, just before the missile was expected to hit the water, some small rockets were launched, which with a huge noise had shot off like fireworks towards the sky to gather the latest weather information for the precise moment of the missile's arrival. Then, all of a sudden, in the sky which was by now dark, above the sea there appeared, like a huge firework, an intensely bright vertical track heading downwards: it splintered into a plethora of secondary tracks, which just for a second lit up all that stretch of sea and sky, as if in a sudden storm-burst. Then, after many seconds of total silence, in the darkness was heard a distant, prolonged bubbling sound.

I wonder whether that evening we too had unwittingly witnessed a missile landing in the sea or whether it was a meteorite, rich in some metal or other, which had been made visible in the clear night sky over Ascension.

This is the second yacht we have seen docking since we came to Ascension. In the morning they came to visit us at the Islander Hostel. Little older than kids, they had been asked to take the yacht of a rich South African from South Africa to England, after he had moved there. There are five of them, three girls and two boys. They are all around twenty-five, three South Africans, a Scots girl and an Australian man. There are only two of them who know about sailing: the captain, South African, and the Scots girl. The others joined them for the fun of the cruise. In the space of around two weeks they sailed from Cape Town to Saint Helena, and in another week from there to Ascension; the other stops planned are Cape Verde, the Canaries and England.

I only want to mention the paternal feelings I felt on seeing them so young, little older than my own children, filled with the same spirit of adventure and the same desire to discover the world, and committed to tackling the adventure of crossing the whole length of the Atlantic.

In the evening we take them to see the nesting turtles, and it is that night that we start to realize why the radios stop transmitting, the night after the green meteorite. The youngsters had seen it too, while sailing towards Ascension, they tell us.

Floriano and I stay with them, sitting in a circle in the sand, and Floriano cannot resist the temptation to hold a little seminar on animal orientation which enthuses all of them, when suddenly Graeme and Paolo pop out of the darkness, in a tremendous state. They had gone to patrol the beach, and found a turtle nesting, one of the ones on which we had attached the radio-transmitter.

We all run to see the turtle: we find her still there, in the process of covering up her nest. There is no doubt: she is definitely the same one that we had attached the PTT to. On the front edge of her carapace, near her head, is the little tag that we had glued on to her with our addresses, telephone numbers, etc. However, the surface of the top of her carapace is totally smooth, there is no sign of anything, none of the various glues, mastics, marks of fibreglass that we had stuck on: basically, the PTT was no longer there.

My friends were bewildered: this was not their first attempt at attaching transmitters to turtles. They had been able to follow them for months via satellite in the China seas and the Indian Ocean. Occasionally some had stopped working before they should, perhaps because they had ended up inside a shark or in some fishing-boat's net, but the majority of them had gone on working for a very long time. They were also worried about the expense: each radio cost £1,300, and the budget was of course limited. So all that money had ended up at the bottom of the sea, without any apparent explanation. Since every tag had an identification number, we could work out precisely which turtle this was: it was the very first one that we had attached a radio to, twelve days previously.

Our South African friends went off thrilled: they had seen turtles laying eggs, even though they did not understand much about what was going on, and in any case they had other plans, despite the Administrator's ban on visitors spending the night on the island. They had met some people of their own age, from the American army, and had been invited to a party. Like all decent parties, for people of that age all over the world, including Ascension, it started at midnight and finished at six in the morning. We would meet them around seven: we were shattered after a night spent patrolling the beach, but they were even worse, after a night of youthful excess, as they headed back towards their boat.

The next night, after spending a day coming up with different hypotheses, we got the confirmation that the most probable explanation was the right one. We found the second turtle that we had attached a radio to: she too had had it attached twelve days previously, she too was identifiable because of the tag, and she too was without any trace of the transmitter. But she had one sign that was not present on the first one: a wound, barely visible yet unmistakable, running across the surface of the back of her neck. My friends, who are turtle experts after all, had no doubts: this was the mark left by a male turtle which had recently mated with her.

The turtle's cumbersome carapace makes mating difficult: it takes place at sea, the male approaches the female from behind, and has a difficult job to restrain her, clinging on to her with his paws, and biting her on the neck. In such circumstances, with the bottom plate of the male grinding against the top of the female's carapace, and considering the bulk of the two creatures, it was easy to foresee the fate of the poor PTT:

ripped off and ground to bits by the erotic endeavours of two turtles mating.

But not all the PTTs were destroyed: the majority of them survived, and allowed us to reconstruct with amazing precision the turtles' homeward journey. But this will be the subject of a later chapter.

23

Despite the efforts and optimism of Captain Brandreth, throughout the whole of the nineteenth century the island was home to only a small military garrison, and no one ever wanted to come and settle there. As time passed it slipped into a long period of torpor, during which, considering the events a century previously, nothing significant happened. Napoleon had died and been forgotten now for some time, the war against the slave-merchants was over, and halfway through the century the Suez Canal opened, thus making it pointless to sail round Africa as a route to the Indies. The West African Squadron, the naval unit detailed to patrol the African coasts, was withdrawn, and the usefulness of garrisoning that little island, so far from anywhere and so infertile, was called more and more into question. However, it was never completely abandoned.

For a century, up to 1922, Ascension belonged to the Navy, to the Lords of the Admiralty, and, since the Navy had no right to deal with matters on dry land but only to look after ships, the island, right from the start of its occupation, was simply declared a ship, a warship, the HMS *Ascension*, under the responsibility of a captain who was in charge of a crew: the small garrison made up of about fifty sailors and Royal Marines and a couple of hundred black workers: Krus.

His Britannic Majesty's warship, throughout its entire existence of a little over one hundred years, was never called upon, not even once, to engage in armed conflict with enemy vessels. And this was lucky because although it had the advantage of being rather difficult to sink, on the other hand it would have been very easy to capture, given the fragile nature of its defences, if anyone had wanted to do so, with even a minimum of determination.

Instead, those who lived on the island in that period had other battles to fight: against boredom, disease, restrictions on expenditure imposed by the Admiralty, nature and self-inflicted excesses.

Up until it was discovered, the island had very little flora and fauna. Perhaps no more than around thirty species of plants: seeds carried by the wind or the birds, which had had the dubious good fortune to take root and to grow sparsely on the highest and most humid parts of the island. As for animals, there were only, though in countless numbers, birds and crabs and, every year for a few months, turtles.

The arrival of humans brought about, right from the start, a series of novelties and instabilities. And it has continued to do so right down to our own times. Each kind of life introduced to the island had to face just two alternatives: to succumb or to survive. The former was the likelier fate. But if chance decreed that the climate and terrain were suitable, then for that species (whether animal or plant) there was every prospect of spreading like wildfire. However improbable this might seem, it was not impossible, for the environment, although difficult, was certainly no more hostile than many others on the globe. And in addition, it had the advantage of not having natural enemies that had to be avoided or competitors with whom to contend for the available resources.

In this kind of environment, every intervention from outside ran the risk of being inept and producing unforeseen consequences. Thus the goats brought there at the beginning destroyed the already scarce vegetation; the rats, which had arrived through no will of their own on board the ships, simply multiplied, while the cats, which had been imported specifically to hunt the rats, found it more profitable to join forces with the rats themselves and devote themselves to preying on birds' nests, which they almost totally eliminated from the main island. Similarly every attempt at establishing gardens or cultivating fields on the summit of Green Mountain was hampered by the immediate spread of parasites (insects, grubs, larvae, etc.) which flourished since they did not have to protect themselves from birds and insect-eating mammals; and attempts at importing the latter failed miserably: the few exemplars of crows, starlings and hedgehogs that survived the long sea-voyage on board ship died out immediately owing to mysterious but inescapable environmental incompatibilities. However, the mynah birds survived, imported from Mauritius in 1879, and their descendants can still be found in huge numbers around Georgetown. Other survivors were some colonies of green canaries which arrived in 1890.

Other animals brought by man escaped his control and ran wild. I have already mentioned the cats, which are still plentiful, and the goats, which have now disappeared. In the past dogs, pigs, rabbits and hens all escaped, but there is now no trace of them. All that remains are the colonies of donkeys, which have been wild for over a century now, wandering around in groups in the dry part of the island, and sheep, which are more common in the green part. The story of the plants is similar: eucalyptus, casuarina trees, Bermuda cypresses, orange and lemon trees, tropical plants, palm-trees, banana-trees, gum-trees, sugar canes, olive-trees, corn, vegetables, bamboos and dozens of other plants were imported in the course of the last century. Many of them have disappeared, some found little niches for themselves where they still survive, like the little olive wood near Devil's Cauldron. Others spread or are still spreading at more or less the same pace.

The eastern part of the island is now all green, while the

western part, which looks at first sight so dry and inhospitable, is undergoing a slow invasion. The volcanic cones are still today completely bare, apart from the odd casuarina tree here and there, but their lower slopes are dotted with sparse bushes, which however were not there in the photographs in the museum taken just a few years ago.

Twenty years ago Georgetown was completely devoid of vegetation, as photographs of the time confirm. Nowadays eucalyptus trees, bougainvilleas, and acacias are almost everywhere. Most of all, though, you find the Mexican thorn tree which I will talk about in the next chapter.

24

A notice-board at the entrance to the Islander Hostel displayed the most important announcements: emergency telephone numbers, the opening times of the two or three shops on the island, the odd edict from the Administrator, and the list of guests expected, with the date of their arrival and departure. Periodically an invisible hand would update the list. As in every inn, boarding house or hotel where the guests are few and nearly always the same (and even more so in a place as remote and forgotten by the rest of the world as this), each new arrival was an object of anticipation and curiosity.

Before I left home, a friend said to me, 'You'll see, you'll meet the weirdest people: the ones that end up on those islands are really strange.' However, the rules on Ascension are too rigorous to allow what are known in English as dropouts to settle there (in German they are called *Aussteiger*; strangely, there is no Italian equivalent of the term), i.e. people who, following the alternative culture of the seventies and eighties, decide to go and live totally cut off from the world.

There are no 'beached' people on this island, the term used for fish thrown up on to the sand by the sea. Everyone here has a job, and is only here for the duration and purpose of that job. Nevertheless, the strangeness of the place is such that it guarantees that you meet very peculiar people.

When we arrived, apart from our own names, there was on the list only that of another British person, who was to leave the next day on the Tristar coming back from Port Stanley. We spent a few hours with him, sitting on the veranda chatting in the early afternoon. He was a British journalist, a pleasant, chubby and slightly sweaty man, who had been sent by his paper to the Falklands and Ascension in order to write some articles on what are the last British colonies, now that Hong Kong was about to go back to China. He explained the rules of the island to us for a bit, but we talked mostly about Italian politics: he was an expert on Europe, and he knew Italy much better than the last remnants of the British Empire.

For a few days a young mulatto Saint Helenian stayed in a room on the ground floor, spending his days indolently waiting for a visa for the Falklands. During that time, every afternoon, while we were trying to recover the sleep we had lost, the only telephone in the hotel would ring. It was positioned at the entrance and had a menacing ring. Mario – that was the name of our young Saint – was never there at that time, so one of us always had to get up to answer it. At the other end of the line there was always a female voice, different every time, but always with the same worried and breathless tone looking for her Mario.

A TV crew from Holland arrived, who had made the same trip and for the same reason as the British journalist. We hardly ever saw them either, as they stayed only two days and were always out filming. They departed leaving behind them an incredible number of empty beer-cans.

Some visitors we never met at all. At a certain point the list contained a couple of names of people whom we never saw, perhaps not without reason.

One day, announced in advance in the Administrator's letter, the entomologist arrived. We met him in the evening, because as on other mornings we slept until late whereas he was immediately out with his beetles, the minute he arrived. Unlike the other people, his presence was never hidden: he had occupied the whole space of the ground-floor veranda with boxes of various sizes covered with a fine tulle net. Inside were dry leaves, small worms and grubs.

He came to see us one evening, when we were right in the middle of a game of chess. We made friends immediately, helped by the bottle of South African wine which he had brought with him. He worked for an agency which dealt with biological control in agriculture using insects.

He had come to Ascension because he had been called in by the Administrator to solve an ecological problem of growing dimensions: the expansion on the island of a prickly bush called the Mexican thorn tree. This plant, whose Latin name is *Prosopis juliflora*, belongs to the Leguminosae family, and is a distant relative of the acacia. Similar bushes are found all over the arid areas of Latin America and they are known in Spanish, and in English, under the generic name of mesquite. The suspicion was that it had been brought by an American soldier at the time of the Falklands War to brighten up his little garden, and it had found the ideal conditions to grow and spread in: the arid climate, varied every few years by brief torrential downpours, the land, the donkeys who eat its seeds and whose faeces spread them, and above all the absence of natural enemies, against which these plants have a fierce struggle in their native land.

These were the very enemies that the entomologist had been called upon to supply. His agency had been consulted some years previously and had sent him to Ascension to reconnoitre. And he had said yes, it was worth trying. Now here he was with the eggs of *Algarobius Prosopis* and of *Nelturius Arizonensis*. He had to keep the larvae in contact with the plant's flowers for a few days, so they could learn to recognize and appreciate them, and then he would release them. If things went well, the first results would be seen in a few years, and in a few decades the spread of *Prosopis juliflora* would be halted. Without pesticides.

*

The evening we met the entomologist, we decided not to go down to the beach. Instead we all went together to the Saints' Club, the only bar open in Georgetown. The Club was a bona fide English pub in the middle of the Atlantic Ocean. The bar itself was in semi-darkness with customers sitting on high stools drinking beer, while all around were little tables with chairs and small couches covered in a red fabric that was worn smooth and stained. On the walls hung yellowing photographs of the ordinary (or rather extraordinary) life of the island: caught fish of every size; the football team which fifteen years previously had beaten the American army team; ships and military aircraft that went back twenty years; the visit by Prince Andrew (on 10 April 1984); and turtles. That evening the place was very crowded, and the amount of beer consumed by everyone, including my friend the entomologist, was prodigious.

With a loquacity unleashed by alcohol, he told me about his journeys all over the world, the last of which was just a few days previously, to Syria, and just before that to Saint Helena, Africa and South America. He introduced me to some Saint Helenian friends whom he knew from his previous visit, and with whom I struck up a very warm though ephemeral friendship. We talked about women, history, politics, the British Empire. We ended up remarking how incredible it was to find ourselves right in the middle of the Atlantic Ocean. By this stage he was almost drunk and began to attack what he saw as the endless history of English arrogance, becoming more and more vitriolic.

As in every English pub, even on that island in the middle of the Atlantic, closing time rigorously follows the same, invariable ritual: at a certain point, indeed at a precise moment, the barman announces it is time for last orders. An opportunity missed by nobody. Then he lowers a shutter with wide interstices which comes down halfway across the counter, separating (and protecting) him from the rest of the customers; and while the latter continue to drink and chat, he gets on imperturbably with cleaning and putting away glasses and bottles. Then, at exactly midnight he tells us that it is time to go home. Everyone knows it is and, though with a heavy heart, they drink the last gulp and leave the pub. I believe that if it were not for these licensing laws the whole of Britain, and Ascension Island too, would in the space of a few weeks collapse into a state of collective *delirium tremens*.

Some time later there arrived on the island a strange trio, who stayed for a couple of days waiting for the ship to take them to Saint Helena.

One was a psychologist, an elderly man, thin and vaguely self-important. The list on the notice-board said he was a professor, and he had that slight superciliousness that is typical of many academics.

The second was an architect, a short, balding man around sixty years old, whose English was as incomprehensible as the professor's was impeccable. He constantly used witticisms, puns and ironic comments that were impenetrable to us, cackling each time for a few seconds, and knocking everything over.

The third person was a woman of indeterminate age, small, slim and rather shy. She was a nurse who had been in Malaysia, had come back to England, then had gone to Malta for ten years before going back to England. She had learned that the Foreign Ministry was looking for someone to take the post of chief nurse on Saint Helena for three years, and she had applied. She left behind a son who was married and a little grandson. She made no mention of the existence of a husband.

Of the trio, this woman was the one who was going to stay longest on Saint Helena. The architect was going for three months. He explained to me, amidst one of his cackles, that he was going to carry out surveys in order to suggest to the government the best way to build something that was (or

seemed) useful for the hospital while costing as little as possible. Lastly, the professor's job was to go and visit the 'problem
children' on the island. He would stay less time than the other
two. Two weeks, just enough time for the ship to arrive in
Cape Town and come back to Saint Helena, and then he would
leave again.

Two days before our departure came the last visitor that we
would share the Islander Hostel with. His name, as it appeared
on the list, suggested without doubt that he was Dutch. When
one morning, on coming down from our rooms, we met a
fair-haired, dazed-looking man, as pink and chubby as a piglet,
who greeted us with a rather guttural 'Good afternoon', we
realized that the Dutchman had arrived on the night flight.

We did not see him for the rest of the day, but when after
dinner we got back from the mess, we met him again. He was
still wearing the same incongruous dark city suit, and seemed
even more crazed than in the morning: the day he had spent
in his room had not refreshed him, but had allowed all the
mosquitoes of the area to take advantage of the new arrival.
(The mosquitoes were initially a major problem for all of us,
but we quickly solved it, for the sake of our survival, each of
us in our own way: repellent creams, anti-mosquito burners,
mosquito-nets on the windows, etc.)

His greeting this time was even more surprising: 'Buona-
sera,' he said to us, this time hitting both the time of day and
our language spot on.

It's a small world! Our Dutch friend not only spoke Italian
well, but also knew our region of Italy very well. His parents
lived in a town just a few kilometres from our city. He was a
writer. He had just finished a book on Bomarzo, that little
medieval village near Viterbo which has a park full of sculpted
monsters, which had been devised by a descendant of the
Orsini family, who had at one time been the rulers of that
area. Not many people in Italy have heard of Bomarzo, and it

is really strange to find yourself discussing it on a mid-Atlantic island.

The Dutchman had come to Ascension to carry out research on the subject of his next book: a Dutch sailor who had apparently been dumped on Ascension in 1725, when the island was still uninhabited. He had committed a sin which on the ships of that period was both rampant and yet abhorred: sodomy.

The story is found in the catalogue of the little museum and in Hart-Davis's book, but neither of them seems to attach too much credence to it. They say that in January 1726 a British Navy vessel, the *Compton*, landed on the island and on the beach were found the remnants of a tent and a diary which had been begun on 5 May of the previous year and whose last entry was on the 14 October. Of its author there was no trace.

It is not up to me to narrate the suffering described in that diary, in which moments of illusory hope are mixed with increasingly dark despair, terrifying solitude, the torments of hunger and thirst, a mounting sense of guilt and a delirious desire to make amends: '14 September: I am becoming a moving skeleton. My strength is entirely decayed. I cannot write much longer. I sincerely repent of the sins I have committed and pray, henceforth, no man may ever merit the misery which I have undergone. [. . .] I now resign my soul to Him that gave it, hoping for mercy.'

In particular it is not my job to leak the results that our co-resident confided to me, based on his researches in the archives of the British and Dutch navies, as he tracked down that unfortunate, perhaps mythical sailor. An initial problem was to establish the historical authenticity of the episode. *The Incredible and True Diary Found by the Crew of HMS Compton on the Coast of Ascension Island*, the sole source of the whole tale, was published in 1726 and follows close on the heels of the publication of a book which from its first appearance became one of the most famous and popular works of all time: *Robinson Crusoe* by Daniel Defoe. Is it legitimate to suspect that it was all a complete fabrication, dreamt up to milk the literary fashion that had been triggered by Defoe's book? Maybe it is.

The story of the sailor abandoned on an island for his homosexuality, whether true or false, was given a more 'partisan' rewriting in the 1980s by a gay writer from San Francisco. However, the latter, said my Dutch friend with some disdain, had not bothered to undertake any historical research, unlike himself.

What truth is there in the terrible tale of the Dutch shipwreck and his diary? If we are to believe my Dutch friend, perhaps there is more to it than is suggested by the books I have consulted.

25

On 20 October 1922 the island of Ascension ceased being considered officially a ship. The military garrison was withdrawn, the munitions detonated, and the rest of the Navy's property sold to a company which for several years had begun to take root on the island: the Eastern Telegraph Company. Already by the end of the nineteenth century the ETC had started dealing with telecommunications via cable, constructing the network that linked Britain and India. Then in 1899 it had supervised the installation of an undersea line which went from Cornwall, via the islands of Cape Verde, Ascension and Saint Helena all the way to Cape Town, just in time for the start of the Boer War.

Ascension had acted as the 'node' where communication routes intersected because of its geographical position, right from the moment of its discovery, when the Portuguese sailors had left on it the first goats 'for posterity', for the availability of future navigators; and later, too, sailors would leave messages there in the hope that other ships, on their way back, would pick them up and take them home.

In the space of a couple of decades at the start of the twentieth century Ascension became, like a spider at the centre of a web, the point on which telegraph cables converged and from which they radiated out: from and to Cape Town, Freetown in Sierra Leone, Porthcurno in Cornwall, Rio de Janeiro and Buenos Aires. The island passed from the Navy to being run by the Commonwealth Ministry, hence by the Governor of Saint Helena. In practice little changed. The by-now-rare British sailors and marines and the not much more numerous Kru workers were replaced by a few dozen employees of the Eastern Telegraph Company and by a hundred or so Saint Helenians who worked for them. Then ETC merged with Marconi and became Cable & Wireless. And since it now dealt not only with undersea cables but also with radio waves, it installed the first radio bridge-head on the island. The headquarters of Cable & Wireless was initially none other than the building which is now the Islander Hostel, in which we stayed.

The only ones whose lives really changed were the turtles. Once sailing ships gave way to steamships, which were faster and easier to control, fewer and fewer vessels stopped at Ascension. The demand for turtle flesh dropped. Once in charge of the island, Cable & Wireless first restricted then banned altogether the hunting of turtles – much to the chagrin of the Admiralty Lords who were reluctant to surrender the privilege of receiving Ascension Island turtle soup on a regular basis, cooked specially for them by the King's Turtle Soup Manufacturer. In order to try and maintain this benefit the Admiralty engaged in a fiercely fought, but pointless and entertaining epistolary contest against Cable & Wireless which lasted a full ten years, as Hart-Davis relates.

Nowadays it is forbidden not only to hunt but even to disturb the turtles. An edict from the Administrator warns that whoever contravenes the ban will be liable to a fine of 'not more than £100 sterling'. (English law imposes a limit on the power authority may exercise in the punishment of citizens. In Italy, by contrast, I think that a similar ban would have the opposite formulation: whoever disobeys this ban will be liable to a fine of no less than 300,000 lire. The citizen is warned: the State can punish him as much as it wants, from a certain limit upwards.)

*

Things changed for everyone when the Second World War broke out. Once more, Ascension was not the scene of any naval, aerial or underwater battle. Despite British anxieties, which were more than justified by the lack of defences (two cannons which had never fired a shot), the island was never attacked. And to think that, in retrospect, it played a crucial role in the war against the German submarines lying in wait for ships in those waters.

In October 1941, in the middle of the war, but before the Americans had become involved, the US government contacted the British (or was it vice versa?) to consider the possibility of establishing a military base on Ascension Island. Similar agreements had been reached for a number of islands (British colonies) in the Caribbean, in exchange for the odd cruiser or other naval warship. Agreement was soon reached, but, says Simon Winchester in his book, the details were never made public. However, the fact is that from that point on a small but significant part of the island became – and still remains today – American to all intents and purposes. In December of that year the Japanese attacked Pearl Harbor and, a few months later, the Americans arrived on Ascension to build the most secret and incredible airport in the world. It was completed in record time, in the space of two months: from 30 March 1942, when the first engineer corps troops disembarked, until 20 May, the day on which the airport was declared operational.

Even allowing for some scepticism for a story told by the victors, the building of that airport, on a lava field, in such adverse conditions and so quickly, was certainly an extraordinary achievement. From that point until the end of the war, something like 20,000 aircraft landed on Ascension: the African war, El Alamein, the British–American landings in Algeria and Sicily, the beginning of the rescue of Europe were all military enterprises made possible partly thanks to the support of aircraft which had stopped on the island. Towards the end of the war, bombers involved even in theatres of war as distant as China, India and Burma stopped on Ascension.

> If you miss Ascension
> Your wife will get a pension.

These lines were well known to the American airmen who took off from Florida or Brazil heading for Ascension. If they missed Ascension they would not have enough fuel to land elsewhere, as there was no land and no airport for a radius of thousands of miles.

In the Atlantic the battle against German submarines continued: all the U-boats came to a sticky end. It was in the vicinity of Ascension that an episode took place that has gone down in the annals of naval warfare as 'the *Laconia* incident'.

In September 1942 a German submarine, U-156, attacked and sank the British liner *Laconia* with 1,800 Italian prisoners of war on board. The U-boat captain, perhaps also because he realized that there were many Italian soldiers amongst the people in the water, asked naval headquarters in Germany for instructions over the radio. The latter ordered him to save the survivors though without endangering the safety of the submarine. The captain brought the submarine to the surface, hoisted the Red Cross flag and began to collect survivors in towed lifeboats, sending out radio messages guaranteeing that he would not interfere with other rescue operations even by the enemy, as long as he himself was not attacked.

However, all this was happening perilously close to the island whose airport, which had just been built, was a secret jealously guarded by the British and Americans. A submarine which had surfaced, albeit engaged in a rescue operation, was still a risk: so, when it was sighted by the reconnaissance planes, it was immediately attacked with no holds barred. Submarine U-156 escaped by diving and cutting adrift the lifeboats. As a consequence of this episode Admiral Dönitz issued the order forbidding any German submarine to rescue survivors from boats they had sunk. Some years later, in the Nuremberg trials, that order was used against Admiral Dönitz himself. Dönitz, however, got off thanks to the evidence of the American Admiral Nimitz, who testified that a similar order had been issued to the US submarines in the Pacific.

26

The days passed and the date of our departure approached, but the Administrator seemed to have forgotten the intention he had had, on the day of our arrival, of inviting us to dinner one evening at his house. And this despite the fact that he was perfectly aware of our presence: partly because Graeme, who looked after our contacts, would periodically go and keep him informed about our researches, and partly because in a town the size of Georgetown everyone knew everything about everyone else.

Then the invitation arrived. We found the envelopes one morning on the desk on the veranda of the Islander Hostel. The address had been written – as was evident from the uneven ink of the characters – with a manual typewriter, by now long out of date; after our names it said: 'c/o The Islander Hostel, Georgetown'. But the card inside was very different in style. At the top stood out, in proud gold relief, the elaborate coat of arms of the British Crown: on the right the lion rampant, on the left the unicorn rampant, in the centre the crown atop the coats of arms of England, Wales, Scotland and Northern Ireland, and the words *Honi soit qui mal y pense* on one side, and on the other, *Dieu et mon droit*. Underneath this emblem, in beautiful printed italics, we were informed that the pleasure of our company was requested by His Honour and His Gracious Consort on Monday 19 May at 7.30 pm at his Residence.

As for dress, the card said: DRESS: ~~INFORMAL/PLAN-TERS~~/CASUAL.

Deciphering this last part of the message caused us to scratch our heads a few times. What 'Planters' meant remained a mystery; mercifully not really relevant, since in any case it was a style of dress which we had been asked not to adopt.

Our entomologist friend intervened. He too had been invited that evening and was more experienced in these niceties than we were. He explained that, with classic English understatement, 'Informal' actually meant terribly formal – dark suit, shirt and tie; 'Planters' (who knows?), something in between; and 'Casual', basically, no tie. This last was exactly what we wanted to know.

The meaning of 'Planters' and the description of the entire range of dress codes envisaged by English manners (and not to be confused with the American code, which is apparently different) were subsequently explained to me by a friend who, as a young man, had for some time worked as a steward on a British cruise ship. Starting from the top, 'Formal' means the maximum of formality: dinner jackets, and the poor Administrator would have had to appear in that case in full uniform, with his three-cornered hat complete with feathers etc. 'Informal', as the entomologist had correctly foreseen, means dark suit, black shoes, white shirt and, of course, a tie. 'Planters' (in its literal sense of planter or settler) means jacket and tie, but brown shoes, no suit and not necessarily a white shirt. 'Casual': not jacket and tie but certainly long trousers. Lastly 'Barbecue' means Bermuda shorts and short-sleeved shirt.

The Administrator's Residence lies almost at the summit of Green Mountain. At one stage it had been 'The San', the sanatorium, the little mountain hospital where sailors and soldiers of the West African Squadron were looked after, usually suffering from yellow fever. We got there as light faded.

A low, square, one-storey house, with its grey stone walls immersed in the deep greenery of the wood. In the shade, on the gravel space in front of it some cars are already parked. The main door is lit by the yellow light of a lantern. It could be an inn in some remote moorland in the heart of England.

Apart from us, His Honour and His Gracious Consort have also invited to dinner: the head of the Cable & Wireless station, who will stand in for the Administrator at functions when the latter goes on holiday to England; an engineer from the BBC; and an RAF officer, each with his respective wife.

The evening goes past very pleasantly. The entomologist talks of his insects, my biologist friends of the turtles, the engineer's wife of how happy their young children are to be going to school at Two Boats instead of in London. The Administrator's wife turns out to be an expert on volcanoes and shows us her collection of minerals.

When it is revealed that I am not really a biologist but a doctor, the Administrator is momentarily shocked and can hardly hide it: has he been deceived? What have I come to do on the island? I reassure him: I have come to accompany my biologist friends, and I too – I lie – do research on turtles. After cocktails, dinner. We are served by two Saint Helenian waitresses, mother and daughter, with black dresses and white aprons, silent and impeccable.

The Administrator tells us about what the future of the island might be. The British will continue to reduce their presence, the Americans will stay on, though also in reduced numbers. A Saint Helenian entrepreneur wants to take over the farm and turn it into a coffee plantation; apparently the climate is ideal for the coffee plant; and moreover Saint Helenian labour costs are so low . . .

There is also the plan to open up the island to tourism: select, up-market tourists who will respect the environment. But investment would be needed, and the Foreign Office (which inherited the island from the Commonwealth Ministry) is not too keen on spending; perhaps the money could be found from European Union funding. But would the Americans agree (though the Administrator does not add this)?

I found on the internet the text of the speech on the state of the 'Dependent Territories' made by the Under-Secretary at the Foreign Office, Baroness Symons of Vernham Dean, in the House of Lords on 11 June 1997. Gibraltar, Hong Kong, the Caribbean, the Falklands, Saint Helena were all dealt with, but on Ascension there was barely a line: 'we are discussing with our American allies the possibility of opening up the island to commercial traffic'.

At table there is talk about other things, the predictable little anecdotes of everyday social life on the island: 'It was such fun the other evening at John's house, listening to his stories . . .'; 'It's been ages since the Waddingtons have had a party . . .'; 'Last time we saw Richard's wife at the Youngs, she said that she wanted to do a course on Chinese cooking, but she has not done anything yet . . .'; 'In any case, I should finish that little book on Saint Helenian cuisine, but I'm still only halfway through . . .', etc.

Inevitably talk comes round to medical subjects. 'You're a doctor, so can I take advantage and ask you . . .' Anyone who has a degree in medicine, and lets it be known, is constantly aware that in this kind of situation there are always likely to be questions like this. We know it is inevitable and we wait for it, dreading when it happens. I am resigned and apprehensive as I await the rest of the question.

27

Once the war was over, Ascension emptied and everything – or almost everything – went back to as it was before. The British and American contingents were withdrawn, the Administrator left as well: he had been sent in his capacity as representative of the Governor of Saint Helena to coordinate activities with the American allies (and to keep an eye on them).

On 31 May 1947 the airport was closed. All that remained was an abandoned runway, a few buildings that it was not worth dismantling and that would become dilapidated on their own, and the employees of Cable & Wireless, who carried on their usual work. Once more peace had returned to the island; even though it was short-lived.

Ten years later, in 1956, the Americans would return, pointing to that 1941 agreement which assigned a part of the island to them. The needs of the Cold War meant that Ascension had once more become useful. It would become the furthest point on the Eastern Range, that stretch of sea that was almost uninhabited, except for a few Caribbean islands, and whose other extremity, 3,000 miles north-west was Cape Canaveral, and inside which the Americans conducted the majority of their experiments to refine their intercontinental missiles.

Ascension was thus used as a base from which to track the course of the missiles launched from Cape Canaveral, while the surrounding waters became a sort of target against which to test the accuracy of those missiles. Then, as time passed, in a more global vision of the planet, the island was used as a strategic point of contact with the satellites hovering over that part of the world; satellites through which one could spy – discreetly, without causing or suffering any annoyance – on what was happening in Africa and South America, the two most turbulent southern continents.

And the island was used not just for spying. During the month of our expedition to Ascension, Mobutu's government fell in what was then called Zaïre. Perhaps it was no accident that right at the time of maximum uncertainty there appeared on the runway two gigantic Galaxies, American military transport aeroplanes. They remained stationary there for a few days, then a few mornings later they disappeared. But by then the political crisis in Zaïre/Congo also seemed to be heading towards a solution.

If for the Americans, who had just become single rulers of the world, it was easy to guess the usefulness of being able to have that island in the middle of the Atlantic, bristling with aerials, with a huge airport and without an indigenous population to have to be accountable to, for the British it was more difficult. The Empire had gone some time ago, and only a few crumbs remained: only a few islands so small and remote as not to be able to afford independence on their own. The last upsurge of national pride had been the Falklands expedition: it had had the definite advantage of calling the bluff of a brutal, corrupt and inefficient military regime, and precipitating its downfall, and it had allowed Mrs Thatcher to prolong her own period of power for several more years. But those times had gone too. The RAF had withdrawn most of its personnel from Ascension, and even the CSO (the semi-secret agency that listens to what is passing through the ether) would also soon go. After the Falklands flare-up, the island seemed to be returning once more to a phase of quiet and oblivion.

28

Ascension Island's turtles: where do they come from, where do they return to and what routes do they follow in their travels?

The first person to broach the problem was the 'father' of marine turtle research, Archie Carr, a professor of zoology from Florida University, who died a few years ago. Between 1960 and 1980 Carr and his fellow researchers had attached an identity tag to an incredible 3,384 turtles which nested on the beaches of Ascension. It promised – in English and in Spanish – a reward of five dollars to whoever found a turtle with a tag and supplied information on the time and place of its finding.

He received data on sixty-six turtles, mostly ones that had ended up in fishermen's nets. They were all from the subequatorial coasts of Brazil, and the majority were from the most easterly part of the coast (and the part nearest Ascension), namely that round the city of Recife, but many others came from as far away as several hundred miles north or south. Despite the numerical limits of that sample – fewer than 2 per cent of the marked turtles were found – those studies suggested that the coasts of Brazil are the main areas of residence of the turtles that every two to three years commute to Ascension Island.

*

After the dark, early days, when one after the other they lost all the first satellite radio-transmitters, my friends had a rethink: we had to be patient. To reduce the risk of losing the radios we had to attach them to those turtles that had reached the end of their laying cycle: the ones that – it was reasonable to suppose – would not spend any more time around the island waiting to mate.

However, there was no external sign to allow us to distinguish the turtles at the end of their nesting cycle from those that would still stay around Ascension. The only way to enhance our chances was to wait a few weeks until the time of year when the normal nesting period ends. At that point, it was legitimate to assume that the (few) turtles we would still find would all be about to lay their last eggs.

This hypothesis proved correct. Paolo went back to Ascension a month later to attach the last radios. We were by now back in Italy, and the data began to flow in, all of it satisfactory: the turtles had left and were continuing to transmit. They continued transmitting for several more weeks. All fifteen turtles which we tracked by satellite headed in their return journey for Brazil.

But the contribution made by this research was not just to validate a pre-existent hypothesis using a different method. The analysis of the turtles' route allowed new information to be added on how the turtles travelled in the sea. As well as new doubts.

The results showed that once they have left the island the turtles immediately head west, taking a route veering slightly south. In this first stretch, their routes are all very close together: it was as if each turtle we tracked, although all leaving at different times, travelled for the first hundred miles or so along the same, identical, invisible corridor. Then as the miles – the hundreds of miles – go past, they tend to diverge, some veering slightly towards north or south, others steering a central course, but all of them maintaining a prevalently westward direction. However, once they have completed about two thirds of the journey and are still a long way off the coast, their routes start to converge again towards their point of arrival: the most easterly point of the Brazilian coast. This behaviour, unless it is due to an extraordinary coincidence, can only be explained apparently in one way: the turtle is able to adjust its own route because it somehow 'notices' the lie of the nearest point of coastline.

What information does the turtle use to adjust its route? It certainly cannot be the sight of the coast, which is still several hundred miles away. Perhaps – my friends maintain – the presence of some smell: some substance coming from the land or carried by the rivers and dissolved in the water or dispersed in the air. But even this is not all that likely since both the winds and the sea currents in that area head mainly in the direction of the coast not towards the open sea.

The turtles swim at an average cruising speed of between 1.5 and 2 miles an hour: a speed that is equivalent to a steady walking pace on dry land, or in the sea to that of a rowing boat, or a pedalo. However, whether that is their actual speed or whether in fact they alternate periods of speed swimming with others of slow swimming or moments when they actually stop to rest (or feed or get their bearings), we cannot tell from satellite telemetry studies: the frequency of soundings is not sufficient to allow us to extract this type of information.

They swim by day and by night, travelling between forty and forty-five miles every twenty-four hours, and it takes them thirty to forty days to reach the Brazilian coastline, which is a distance of some 1,400 miles.

They swim irrespective of whether there is daylight or not, whether there are clear skies or not, and whether the sun, stars or moon are visible, thus proving that, unlike other migrating creatures such as many types of birds, turtles do not use, or do not need, these heavenly bodies for orientation purposes. Nor are they put off when they are prevented from using the earth's magnetic field as reference point.

This last was one of the most interesting aspects of my friends' research. We attached to different parts of the carapace of seven of the fifteen turtles small but powerful magnets, using a particularly ingenious system. The magnets were not fitted directly on to the carapace, but through semi-rigid metal holders several centimetres long which allowed them to oscillate to a certain extent when the creature was moving, thus creating around it a magnetic field of greater intensity than that of the earth's magnetic field, and also one that could be constantly varied. Furthermore, in order to avoid the magnets being fixed permanently to the turtles, part of their holder was made of a metal that would be corroded by seawater and which after around four weeks would cause the magnets to come away from the turtles' bodies. Well, the routes taken by these seven turtles were indistinguishable from those of the other 'non-magnetic' turtles, despite the fact that the seven had magnets with them, and even more importantly despite the widely held view that marine turtles, along with many other animals, orientate themselves by means of the earth's magnetic field, which they use not only to recognize the four cardinal points, but also to establish their own position on earth. A widely held view, but one which, according to my friends, has never been completely proven.

The idea that turtles used a kind of internal compass to be able to orientate themselves was indeed anything but justified. It stemmed from the analyses of a group of American researchers, who had shown that if baby turtles were placed in a tub and allowed to swim freely, they tended all to swim spontaneously in one direction, changing it only when they were exposed to a magnetic field.

Perhaps, say my friends, there is not necessarily any contra-

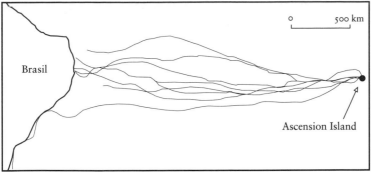

Reconstruction of the routes followed by the turtles from Ascension to Brazil. The traces of some turtles mysteriously disappear before arrival.

diction between the fact that baby turtles use information from the earth's magnetic field to maintain for a brief stretch their course towards the open sea, before they have exhausted their scarce energy reserves and start to let themselves be pulled along by the currents, and the fact that adult turtles are just as capable of discovering the route home halfway across the Atlantic, even when their perception (if they have any) of the earth's magnetic field is impeded.

What the mechanisms are, then, that allow turtles to keep on course in the middle of the ocean still remains a mystery. A mystery that borders on the incredible if one bears in mind the precision with which they manage to keep to an almost straight course in the open sea, despite currents, winds, storms and the apparent absence of any point of reference. Travelling day and night non-stop for forty days at the speed of an average pedalo.*

---

* My biologist colleagues have now shown that turtles find their way to Ascension Island by sniffing air. This follows studies in which turtles were taken from the beach after nesting and then dropped in water again at some distance from the island: those dropped to the leeward of the island swam towards Ascension; those dropped to the windward returned to Brazil. (S. G., 2002.)

29

Three times I went up Green Mountain, each time swearing it would be the last. From Two Boats the road rises brusquely, winding up the mountainside. The climb is short, scary and dangerous. You are met by a series of sheer mountain bends, at each of which the car seems as if it is not going to make it, but each time whoever is driving manages at the last moment to force the engine to make one final effort and get the car round the hairpin.

Meanwhile the environment around you changes rapidly. The almost desert-like vegetation of Two Boats becomes more lush: bushes, plants, flowers of all kinds, trees that become more and more luxuriant and majestic, while the view broadens out in all directions. We get to the end of the road with the engine boiling over and smoke pouring out of the bonnet: before setting back down again, we discover each time that the water in the radiator has completely evaporated.

We are about 2,200 feet above sea-level and there are little more than 300 feet to go to the summit, but it can only be reached on foot. Just after the car park there is the farm, which has always been and still is the only spot on the island where a bit of agriculture and livestock-breeding are practised. At one stage this was done by marines who had become farmers; now it is done by some Saint Helenians, employees of AIS, the consortium that supplies most of the services to the island.

It is quite disorienting coming up here: you leave the car

under a forest of gigantic banana-trees and other tropical plants, turn round a corner and you find yourself facing a typical English farmhouse. On one side is a perfect, very green lawn, with a tree on it from which hangs a swing, on the other lies a garden with rows of roses and raspberries hiding the vegetable lots. A bit further up is the pigsty, with a sow and a great crowd of piglets both terrified and deeply curious. The wind carries familiar but unlikely sounds for a tropical island in the middle of the ocean: a cock crowing, and the sound of cow-bells. As we climb we meet a Saint Helenian in his working-overalls; in front of him trots a little pig which he guides with a stick, prodding it gently on its sides.

From here the view covers the north-western part of the island: the volcanoes, the fields of lava, the airport and all around the immensity of the sea.

The third time I went up here was on our last day, with our friend the entomologist, to have a long walk along Elliot Path and to say our farewells to the island. Built in 1839 and opened by Admiral Elliot, head of the naval squadron patrolling the west coast of Africa, it is a long, flat path running just under the summit of Green Mountain, at an altitude where you only rarely find the clouds which often hide the summit. From Elliot Path a few sailors on watch could survey the entire coastline and spot any pirates or other enemy ships trying to land. During the Second World War the path was widened: some people say that you can still see the tracks of an American jeep that left the path and plunged down the side of the mountain.

We leave on our right a small valley covered with slabs of grey stone. At the top it opens out like a fan, and at the bottom it converges into a cone: this is the system for collecting rain water that was built in 1881 and on which the survival of the island depended until a few decades ago.

On our left is the path leading to Dew Pond, the little pool at the top of the mountain, on the site of the ancient crater, in which live a colony of goldfish, taken up there heaven knows when or by whom. All around there is a thick bamboo grove.

Even to this day, four times a year, one of the craziest foot-races imaginable takes place on Ascension. All fit adults on the island have to – or are expected to – take part. The race starts from Georgetown on the beach beside the Turtle Ponds; at the start you have to bathe your hand in the seawater, and then race up to the top of Green Mountain (those who are able) and dip the same hand in the water of Dew Pond. The race was invented to keep the sailors and soldiers stationed on the island in the last century occupied, but fortunately it did not take place in the month we were there.

For a long stretch our path advances as though in a ditch between two walls of very dense vegetation more than six feet high. Above us is the amazing blue of the sky, where huge clouds rush by at high altitude. Every now and again the vegetation becomes less dense, occasionally disappearing altogether, opening up dizzying vistas. We are on the side exposed to the wind, looking south-east on to the green unin-habited side of the island. Down below there is no trace of humanity, except for the road leading to the NASA station.

Because of the close relationship that links botany to insects, the entomologist also knows a lot about plants, and he rattles off their Latin names to me though he pronounces them in an English accent. Needless to say, of that torrent of names I cannot remember one. There were agave plants originating from Madagascar; one herbaceous plant in particular was from the Himalayas and was spreading like wildfire on the plateaus of many oceanic islands (Hawaii, the Fiji Islands, etc.); and an extremely rare form – it seems – of cedar tree which is local to Bermuda.

We come to a tunnel which was built to avoid the most dangerous precipices, the entomologist reassures me (though he is only partly successful). After a few moments we are in total darkness. All we can see is the light of the exit fifty yards away, and as we have no torches we advance without the slightest idea of where we are putting our feet. The entomologist boldly and chattily leads the way, while I grope behind him feeling my way on sticky, uneven ground that I cannot see. We emerge with relief and notice that suddenly the landscape around is totally different.

We have come round the most easterly spur and at this point are looking northwards. The vegetation has changed: what is missing is the comforting cushion of bushes that protected us down below. We are now exposed: nothing but grass on slopes of vertiginous steepness. Above us, our view reaches as far as the clump of bamboo wood at Dew Pond; beneath us is the sheer drop and the north-eastern portion of the island, totally inaccessible as no road runs there; in front of us is the Weather Post, the second highest mountain (or volcano) on Ascension, hiding the tiny Boatswain Bird island, a sanctuary for the majority of the seabirds; beside us on the right is Cricket Valley, while on the left is the imposing crater of the Devil's Cauldron.

We are now on the way back down; below us is the start of the dry, desert-like part of the island, and you can already glimpse the giant pylons of the BBC's Atlantic Station at English Bay; the volcanic outlines of the Sisters, Broken Tooth and Hollow Tooth, Perfect Crater and lastly, in the distance, the by now familiar profile of Cross Hill, behind which shortly the sun will dip into the sea.

We quicken our pace: in a few hours we will have to have our suitcases packed, ready to be taken to the airport by the duty policeman and to take off into the night aboard the Tristar coming in from the Falklands. At the moment of departure I will be overcome – I know this already – by a sort of longing for omnipotence, a kind of melancholy consciousness of my own irremediable lack of permanence, that seizes me every time I leave somewhere to return home, from some distant, unusual place where – I am well aware – I will never return.

Epilogue

My friends went back to Ascension to attach other transmitters to the turtles and to continue their researches into their movements.

From what Paolo and Floriano told me nothing seems to have changed there: the same sleepy atmosphere in Georgetown, slightly tinged with melancholy, the same people, the same empty beaches, the same isolation. Two weekly flights for the few who have a travel permit or the ship that calls in once a month.

But in reality some things are changing. A huge dish aerial has been installed at the NASA station, where the older aerials had followed the descent of the first man on the moon. This allows them to receive BBC television programmes live. The *Islander* has been updated, now printing colour photographs and devoting two whole pages to TV programmes. Funding to modernize the Exiles' Club will perhaps be granted, and Graeme has found the money to employ two Saint Helenians to check and protect the turtles that land on the beaches.

Now that the thorny question of Hong Kong has been settled, the remaining British colonies will be accorded a different status. Discussions with the American partners have ended and shortly the airport will – perhaps – be open to normal air traffic. There is talk of opening a small airport on Saint Helena, which would allow it to be linked to Ascension and with the rest of the world. As for the museum, the director has gone back to the USA, and thence to Alaska, but a new director will look after it. The Administrator is also approaching retirement and has written a book on the turtles which he hopes to publish. In the near future, but we do not know exactly when, the island will open up to tourism. 'It will be a gain for the world, but it will lose its status as a "non-existent place".' To what extent this is good news, I cannot say.*

---

* Since I finished this book in October 1999 some limited tourism has begun in Ascension; in addition, and equally importantly, the legal situation of the island – as well as of that of the other overseas territories – is about to change: legislation is just going through that will grant British citizenship to the Saints and enable them to develop private enterprise and ownership of property on the island. Information on the development of Ascension's near future will be found, for those who are curious about it, in the web-pages listed in the Webography at the end of the book. (S. G., January 2002.)

Appendix

SAINT HELENA

Saint Helena is unique: it is at the same time one of the best known and one of the least known islands on earth. Everyone has heard of Saint Helena, but very few know anything about it, apart from the story of Napoleon, and hardly anyone has ever been there. 'The best kept secret in the world' is what they say of Saint Helena.

I have not been to Saint Helena either, but it is almost as if I knew the island. Saint Helena (which here is pronounced Saint Heleena, with the accent on the penultimate syllable) looms large on Ascension. More than a third of Ascension's residents come from there: harbour workers, policemen, the fire-fighters at the American base, employees in the various service industries, from shops and the petrol station to road maintenance, telecom employees, electricians, the cooks in the mess where we ate, the woman who came twice a week to tidy our bedrooms – all of them came from Saint Helena.

If Ascension is remote, Saint Helena is even more so. It has no airport, no real harbour, and is served by only one regular ship, also called the *Saint Helena*, which calls in once – or if all goes well, twice – a month. The ship plies between Cardiff in Wales and Cape Town in South Africa, stopping at Tenerife, Ascension, Saint Helena and, once a year, Tristan da Cunha. From Cardiff to Saint Helena it takes about two weeks, but from Cape Town it only takes five days.

Slightly larger than Ascension (surface area forty-seven square miles against Ascension's thirty-five square miles), Saint Helena is also different in one major respect: being in more temperate latitudes, it has water. It has been continuously inhabited since 1659, by the English, except for a very brief interval of a few years when the Dutch came. Amongst its first settlers were some Londoners who had lost everything in the great fire of 1666. In the past it had a certain importance (apart from Napoleon) as a stop-off point from and to the Indies before the opening of the Suez Canal. It also had some manufacturing industry (flax). But now it has been forgotten.

At the very time we were on Ascension, Saint Helena attracted the attention of newspaper reports. Even some Italian papers devoted a small paragraph to this. Apparently there were demonstrations on the island against the Governor and some rioting: the situation was said to be 'tense'. When we read this news a few days later in the *Islander*, which devotes four or five pages to Saint Helenian affairs, the situation seemed less dramatic: two members of the island's council had resigned, the Governor had declared new elections and had gone off on holiday to Britain. The problems, however, were genuine and had existed for a long time: they were twofold, the economic situation and the failure to grant British citizenship.

Since the collapse of the island's last resource, the cultivation of flax, Saint Helena has not had a proper economy: it produces a small amount of tinned tuna which is very good, and is on sale in the Ascension supermarket, and some coffee, which is said to be excellent, but is 'the dearest coffee in the world'. Saint Helena lives on subsidies.

The other burning issue is that the Saints do not have British citizenship. They used to have it, but in 1981 it was removed by the Westminster government. When Mrs Thatcher realized that the Chinese were serious and that Britain would have to surrender Hong Kong, in order to prevent a mass exodus from that colony to the UK, she decided to deprive its inhabitants of British citizenship; and, not being able to do this just for Hong Kong, she extended the 'Nationality Act' to all the other inhabitants of the dependent territories, few though they were. The consequences are significant: unlike what happened in the last French colonies, which became 'Overseas Départements and Territories' (New Caledonia, Martinique, Reunion Islands, Tahiti, etc.), the citizens of Saint Helena have to have a permit to live and work in Britain.*

When the return of Hong Kong to China was imminent, that was the moment to revive the question, 'because the Saint Helenians', wrote the Reverend Nicholas Turner, of Saint Helena, 'are not poor little natives utterly devoted to Britain. They are as British as the inhabitants of England. They are English and of mixed ethnic origin, just like in the rest of Britain.'

A total of 5,500 people live there, called Saints. Over the centuries, Europeans, Africans, Indians, Chinese and Polynesians (sailors, shipwrecked mariners, settlers, emancipated slaves, soldiers of the garrison, prostitutes, merchants . . .), settled there and all immediately mixed, giving rise to a heterogeneous population in which the varied miscellany of specific characteristics of each single race has produced the most unpredictable outcomes. You find all possible gradations of colour of skin coupled with all different kinds of body types: blacks with typical white features, or typical Asian features, whites with typical black features and so on. I already mentioned the young black policeman with almond-shaped blue eyes who came to fetch us at the airport.

The place where we got to know the Saints most closely was in their mess. It was opposite the Islander Hostel: all you had to do was cross the street to reach the low building where they ate.

* Things have changed markedly since this book was completed in October 1999: see footnote on p. 139. (S. G., January 2002.)

One of the reasons why Floriano was salivating at the prospect of the trip to Ascension was because down there he was sure he would eat fish every day. How wrong he was. No cuisine is more typically English than what we were offered at the Saints' mess on Ascension. Shepherd's pie, Yorkshire pudding, potato pancakes, kidney pie, Banbury cakes: these were some of the names on the menu we were given. As an alternative there was a dish with an unpronounceable name, based round curried meat: beef, mutton, chicken, potatoes, all flavoured with curry paste, Worcester sauce, tomato ketchup, and blueberry jam.

I know, wherever you go in the world, you find French, Italian, Chinese, Indian, Arabic, Japanese, Spanish, Vietnamese, Afghan, even German, Russian, Turkish, Hungarian, Brazilian and any other kind of restaurant: but it is almost impossible to find a restaurant serving typical British food outside Britain. Having spent a month on Ascension, allow me to say that our fears were unjustified. We ate very well at the Saints' mess.

It really could be said of the Saint Helenians that they are more British than the British, because their sense of loyalty to and identification with the motherland is very strong. You can see this, apart from their cuisine, in their dress, their favourite sports (cricket especially), in their attachment to the Royal family (in shops and offices – but even, they tell me, in the good sitting-room in every house – there is a photograph of the Queen), in their habits.

Shortly before our departure the *Saint Helena* stopped at Ascension. In the morning, when I went down to the harbour, it was there in the bay. It had arrived the night before and was to leave late that afternoon, after loading and unloading. A huge raft plied between the harbour and the ship, the jetty was cluttered with crates and an enormous red crane, positioned at the end of the pier, was hoisting a lorry to transfer it on to the raft. Five or six workers in blue overalls, gloves and hard hats were busy, along with a foreman, with the lorry, shouting orders and warnings to each other and to the crane operator high up in his cabin. The scene was being watched by a policeman and a few curious onlookers: the usual group of local loafers and the odd traveller who had arrived in the ship and was waiting to sail off again for Saint Helena. Suddenly, as if by magic, everything stopped, including the lorry which was in mid-air. The crane operator climbed down from his cabin, the dock-workers removed gloves and hard hats, the policeman (who seemed to be there for precisely this purpose) headed towards a small table on which there stood a large, cylindrical metal container from the bottom of which projected a tap, and he began to pour tea for everyone. He even offered some to me. For a few minutes we stayed calmly drinking our tea in the sun and wind of the morning. Then everyone stirred and went back to work as before. I looked at my watch: yes, it is now ten past eleven, tea-break is over.

Webography

We all know that the internet, the web, is a kind of dynamic building, forever subject to new constructions, additions, demolition and face-lifts. It is therefore likely that some of the web addresses quoted are no longer accessible when the reader tries to locate them.

Chapter 1

One of the best documented sites for images of Ascension is at:
http://eclipse.span.ch/live.htm

Its author is Olivier R. Staiger, a passionate photographer of celestial phenomena (eclipses, stellar conjunctions, etc.). In April 1998, exactly a year after us, he visited Ascension, the only place from which to see what is apparently a very rare phenomenon: the simultaneous eclipse of both Venus and Jupiter by the Moon. Going through his web pages, as I discovered after finishing this book, you can run through a kind of parallel virtual journey. For instance, at the address:
http://eclipse.span.ch/20ap98.htm you can actually leave from Brize Norton.

Chapter 2

Images of the Ascension airport are under:
http://eclipse.span.ch/21ap98.htm
Curiously, at the same site you can find a view from the aeroplane window at dawn just like the one described here.
Images of wind generators can be viewed at:
http://www.doe.gov/energy100/world/51.html and at
http://www.publiconline.co.uk/mcgrath/views.htm

Chapter 3

An interesting site from which to start to navigate the field of geographical discoveries is:
http://www.win.tue.nl/cs/fm/engels/discovery/

Chapter 4

Those wishing a (virtual) visit to the Administrator should go to:
http://www.ascension-island.gov.ac/

Chapter 5

What is happening at Ascension harbour can be seen 'in real time' by going to:
http://www.the-islander.org.ac/webcam/
The web-page is linked to a web-cam placed on the harbour-master's window-sill. In practice, this is an automatic camera which records and updates the images automatically every three minutes, from 7 a.m. to 7 p.m.

Chapter 6

There are interesting sites on William Dampier at:
http://www.athenapub.com/damp1.htm and
http://pacific.vita.org/pacific/dampier/dampier.htm

On the links between Alexander Selkirk's memoirs and Daniel Defoe's *Robinson Crusoe*, you can consult:
wy.essortment.com/alexanderselkir__rehj.htm

For the history of phantom islands and related legends, I refer you exceptionally to a 'paper' source, rather than an internet site: D. J. Johnson's book, *Phantom Islands*.

An ancient and somewhat fanciful map of Ascension ('Vera Effigies et Delineatio Insulae Ascensio . . .') can be found at:
http://geowww.ou.edu/~bweaver/Ascension/gtown.htm

Chapter 7

Some photographs of Georgetown can be viewed on one of Barry Weaver's web-pages:
http://geowww.ou.edu/~bweaver/Ascension/gtown.htm

For an image of Ascension's post office, see:
http://www.ascension-island.gov.ac/postoffice.htm

The most recent stamps franked at Ascension can be seen at:
http://www.ascension-island.gov.ac/ascstamps.htm

Those interested in a visit to the Exiles' Club can go to:
http://eclipse.span.ch/24april98.htm

Chapter 8

A representation of continental movements in the various geological eras can be seen at:
http://vishnu.glg.nau.edu/rcb/globaltext.html

You can consult a map of the oceanic ridges at:
http://volcano.und.nodak.edu/vwdocs/vwlessons/volcano_types/spread.htm

Darwin's text and some of his original illustrations can be found at:
http://pauillac.inria.fr/~clerger/Darwin.html

On Ascension's volcanoes, see:
http://geowww.ou.edu/~bweaver/Ascension/ai-geol.htm

For Krakatoa, see:
http://volcano.und.nodak.edu/vwdocs/volc_images/southeast_asia/indonesia/krakatau.html

Photographs of the eruption of Mount Pelée can be seen at:
http://volcano.und.nodak.edu/vwdocs/volc_images/img_mt_pelee.html

Some very beautiful photographs of Surtsey are at:
http://www.islandia.is/hamfarir/jardfraedilegt/eldgos/surtsey.html (the text is all in Icelandic).

Another site on Surtsey island is:
http://www.soest.hawaii.edu/GG/ASK/surtsey.html

On the young island of Lahtayikee, in the Tonga archipelago, consult:
http://www.mclink.it/n/infocity/archivio/scienzamar96.htm

Information on the vicissitudes of Ferdinandea can be found at:
http://www.geocities.com/Heartland/Acres/9369/isolaferdinandea.htm

Chapter 9

A brief history of Ascension's turtle ponds, written by the Administrator, is at:
http://www.the-islander.org.ac/1431.htm

Chapter 10

An old photograph of a captured turtle at the turtle pond is to be seen at:
http://www.heritage.org.ac/Ross6.htm
Typical images of the volcanic landscapes of the island can be found at several addresses, amongst which are:
http://eclipse.span.ch/22ap98later%20in%20the%20 morning.htm
http://geowww.ou.edu/~bweaver/Ascension/ai-tour.htm
http://www.websmith.demon.co.uk/AscensionIsland/ index.html#FIRSTIMP

Chapter 11

For information and images of the eruptions at Montserrat, see:
http://volcano.und.nodak.edu/vwdocs/current_volcs/ montserrat/montserrat.html
http://www.geo.mtu.edu/volcanoes/west.indies/soufriere/
Photos of John Hobson, Ascension Island's dentist, and of Paddy, his dog, are at:
http://eclipse.span.ch/25april98.htm
For perspectives on Ascension's possible future, see:
http://www.fco.gov.uk/news/newstext.asp?3861#recommends

Chapter 12

On the British government agency CSO (Composite Signals Organization), one can consult the site:
http://www.fas.org/irp/world/uk/gchq/index.html
On Sunday mornings you can watch the arrival of the fishing boats through the web-cam mentioned in the note to Chapter 5,

unless there are loading or unloading operations going on. You can often see the tanker in the background.

Chapter 13

Photographs of turtles at night on the sand at Long Beach can be found in the already mentioned site run by Olivier R. Staiger at: *http://eclipse.span.ch/april21evening.htm*
   Other sites for marine turtles are: *http://www.seaturtle.org/* and *http://www.turtles.org*

Chapter 14

The Annals of Tristan da Cunha can be downloaded (but not printed) from the web at: *http://www.btinternet.com/~sa_sa/tristan_da_cunha/ annals_main.html*

Chapter 15

On the American military base on Ascension, see: *http://geowww.ou.edu/~bweaver/Ascension/usbase.html*
   The American military base can also be visited by going to: *http://eclipse.span.ch/24april98.htm* (it even includes the signpost with the distances in all directions).
   A quite significant photograph of the geomagnetic observatory on Ascension is visible at: *http://www.geomag.bgs.ac.uk/ascension.html*
   Images of the Deep Space Station, Ascension Island, can be found at: *http://deepspace.jpl.nasa.gov/dsn/history/album/dsn41.html* and *http://www.scouts.org.ac/nasa_site.htm*

For an image of Cricket Valley see:
http://geowww.ou.edu/~bweaver/Ascension/cricket.htm
On crabs and other indigenous invertebrates on Ascension one can consult:
http://www.rspb.org.uk/wildlife/default.asp

Chapter 16

An exhaustive site on the evolution of turtles is:
http://www.ucmp.berkeley.edu/anapsids/anapsidalh.html

Chapter 17

Today you can read the *Islander* on-line at:
http://www.the-islander.org.ac/

Chapter 18

For an image of the Bonetta cemetery you can consult:
http://geowww.ou.edu/~bweaver/Ascension/comfort.htm
Images of the island in period lithographs can be found at:
http://www.telepath.com/bweaver/allen/allen.htm
They are by Lieutenant William Allen who was in service on the island in that time.

Chapter 19

The text of Darwin's book can be consulted at:
http://www.literature.org/authors/darwin-charles/the-voyage-of-the-beagle/chapter21.html

Images of Ascension Island birds can be found under:
http://geowww.ou.edu/~bweaver/Ascension/boatbird.htm

Chapter 20

Sisters' Peak, Two Boats and Broken Tooth can be seen, start-ing from:
http://geowww.ou.edu/~bweaver/Ascension/ai-tour.htm
The worst golf-course on the planet can be viewed by going to:
http://eclipse.span.ch/22ap98later%20in%20the%20 morning.htm
In another page on the same site can be seen the Ariane site:
http://eclipse.span.ch/22ap98afternoon.htm

Chapter 21

Images of turtles with the PTT attached are available at:
http://cccturtle.org/attach_perd.htm
http://www.kustem.edu.my/seatru/
http://www.tamar.org.br/sat_fotos.htm
Those interested in satellite telemetry studies can consult:
http://www.argosinc.com/
The page devoted to animal migration is under:
http://www.argosinc.com/docs/biology.htm

Chapter 22

The history of the Eastern Test Range, renamed for some years now as 45.Space Wing, is under:
http://www.fas.org./spp/military/program/6555th/ 6555c3-2.htm

Information on MILS (Missile Impact Location System) can be found at:
http://www.pidc.org/hydrobox/NetworkInformation/ Ascension/summary.html

Chapter 23

On Ascension's vegetation, you can find something at:
http://eclipse.span.ch/22ap98afternoon.htm
A comparison of how the Garrison looked at the beginning of the twentieth century with how Georgetown is today can be made by looking at the photographs that belonged to R. H. Morgan, the Royal Marine Commandant of Ascension from 1905 to 1908. The photographs are at:
http://www.heritage.org.ac/HS6.htm If you click on the photographs you can see the same scenes as they appear today.

Chapter 24

The Mexican thorn trees can be seen under:
http://eclipse.span.ch/22ap98afternoon.htm

Chapter 25

For the events leading up to the birth of Cable & Wireless and for the history of its radio station which has been working for a hundred years on the island, you can consult:
http://www.atlantis.co.ac
Information on 'the *Laconia* incident' is at:
http://uboat.net/ops/laconia.htm

Chapter 26

On the project to start cultivating coffee on Ascension, see the web-page:
http://www.theeastindiacompany.com/coffee3html

Chapter 27

The history of the Falklands/Malvinas War can be found on several sites, amongst which are:
http://www.falklands-malvinas.com/chronolo.htm and *http://www.yendor.com/vanished/falklands-war.html*

Chapter 28

Two sites dealing with Archie Carr's work are:
http://www.flmnh.ufl.edu/natsci/herpetology/turtcroclist/fore.htm and *http://www.turtles.org/archie/htm*
    A series of very beautiful underwater photographs of green turtles near Ascension can be seen at:
http://www.seaturtle.org/mtrg/projects/ascension/undersea.shtml
    Some of the routes followed by the turtles can be seen at:
http://www.swan.ac.uk/biosci/acadstaff/turtle.htm

Chapter 29

Those wanting to take a virtual trip to Green Mountain should go to:
http://eclipse.span.ch/upgreenmountain.htm and its following pages (you can even go into the tunnel).

Epilogue

Since the first drafting of this book, virtual accessibility (and to a minor extent real accessibility) to the island has increased enormously.

The internet has come to Ascension as well, and it now has its own identifying code (ac). Amongst the sites about the island you can visit, the most important are: the Administrator's Office (*http://www.ascension-island.gov.ac/*), which provides information also on how to apply to visit the island – this has now become possible even though it is not a simple operation (*http://www.ascension-island.gov.ac/visitors.htm*); Cable & Wireless (*http://atlantis.co.ac/*); AIS (*http://www.ainsa.co.uk*); and above all the newspaper the *Islander* (*http://www.the-islander.org.ac/*).

As mentioned in several footnotes, things at least from the official point of view are changing quickly these days. Those who like to be kept informed may consult one of the following related pages of the official website of the Foreign and Commonwealth Office:

http://www.fco.gov.uk/news/dynpage.asp?Page=10866&Theme=36&Template=999
http://www.fco.gov.uk/news/keythemehome.asp?36
http://www.fco.gov.uk/news/newstext.asp?3861#recommends

The best sites for links to navigate and explore the island are:

http://www.atlantis.co.ac/ascension__links.htm
http://www.websmith.demon.co.uk/AscensionIsland/links.htm
http://geowww.ou.edu/~bweaver/Ascension/ai.htm

Two recent visitors have put on the web an account of their journey and many images:

http://www.websmith.demon.co.uk/AscensionIsland/index.html#FIRSTIMP
http://eclipse.span.ch/live.htm

A site very rich in Ascension's history, offering a wealth of information and pictures, is:
http://www.heritage.org.ac/index.htm

Finally some addresses where you can meet and chat online with other interested persons, as well as be kept up to date with all the news:

http://www.ascension-island.gov.ac/visitorsbook.htm#
visitors

http://www.ascension-island.gov.ac/visitorsbook.htm#
discussion and

http://www.ascension-island.gov.ac/visitorsbook.htm#
mailing

Appendix

A good point from which to start 'exploring' Saint Helena is the official Saint Helena government website:
http://www.sainthelena.gov.sh/

Other interesting sites are:
http://geowww.gcn.uoknor.edu/www/ascension/sh.htm and
http://ourworld.compuserve.com/homepages/
sthelenainstitute/index.html

On the coffee grown on Saint Helena you can consult:
*http://www.theeastindiacompany.com/coffee_*
introduction.html

Bibliography

Ascension at War (Wood Norton: The Historical Society, BBC, 1997)

M. Ashmole, P. Ashmole, *Natural History of St Helena and Ascension Island* (Oswestry, Shropshire: Anthony Nelson, 2000)

A. Carr, 'The Ascension Island green turtle colony', *Copeia* (1975), 547–55

A. Carr, *The Sea Turtle: So Excellent a Fishe* (Austin: University of Texas Press, 1992)

F. J. Clarke, 'Ascension Island: an engineering victory', *National Geographic* (May 1944), 623–40.

Gallery of Photographs: Old Documents and Other Memorabilia, Catalogue (Ascension Island: Ascension Island Historical Society, 1985)

D. Hart-Davis, *Ascension: The Story of a South Atlantic Island* (New York: Doubleday, 1973)

D. S. Johnson, *Phantom Islands of the Atlantic* (New York: Walker and Co., 1996)

J. Keilor, *Memories of Ascension 1929–31* (Newmarket: Miles Apart, 1997)

A. Layolo, G. Lombardi, *L'isola in capo al mondo* (Rome: Nuova ERI, 1994)

K. J. Lohmann, *et al.*, 'How sea turtles navigate', *Scientific American*, vol. 266, 1 January 1992, 82–9

P. Luschi, *Migrazione ed orientamento delle tartarughe*

marine: esperimenti di telemetria satellitare (Doctoral thesis: University of Pisa, 1993–6)

P. Luschi, G. C. Hays, C. Del Seppia, R. Marsh, F. Papi, 'The navigational feats of green sea turtles migrating from Ascension Island investigated by satellite telemetry', *Proceedings of the Royal Society of London, B (Biological Sciences)*, 265 (1998), 2279–84

P. L. Lutz, J. A. Musick (eds), *The Biology of Sea Turtles* (New York: CRC Press, 1997)

R. Marx, 'Ascension Island', *Oceans* (November, 1975), 38–43

G. Melega, *L'isola più isola: Viaggio a Sant'Elena* (Milan: Scheiwiller, 1993)

J. A. Mortimer, A. Carr, 'Reproduction and migrations of the Ascension Island green turtles (Chelonia Mydas)', *Copeia* (1987), 103–13

J. E. Packer, *A Concise Guide to Ascension Island* (Ascension Island: Ascension Island Historical Society, 1968)

F. Papi, 'Migrazione e orientamento nelle tartarughe marine', *Le Scienze*, 338 (1996), 82–5

F. Papi, R. Mencacci, 'The green turtles of Ascension Island: a paradigm of long-distance navigational ability', *Rendiconti Fisici dell'Accademia dei Lincei*, series IX, vol. 10 (1999), 109–19

D. Quammen, *The Song of the Dodo: Island Biogeography in an Age of Extinction* (New York: Touchstone, Simon and Schuster, 1996)

B. Stonehouse, *Wideawake Island: The Story of the B. O. U. Centenary Expedition to Ascension* (London: Hutchinson, 1960)

S. Winchester, *Outposts: The Sun Never Sets: Travel to the Remaining Outposts of the British Empire* (New York: Simon and Schuster, 1991)

L. B. Young, *Islands: Portraits of Miniature Worlds* (New York: W. H. Freeman and Company, 1999)